BURY ME
IN MY
BATHING
SUIT

*Essays on life, grief
and unexpected joybursts*

SAMI GREENFIELD

ISBN: 978-1-946694-94-2

What you're searching for isn't out there, it's in here, Hiccup."
— Astrid, How to Train a Dragon

Todd, Tyler, Mason, and Simba

Thank you for your endless love and patience as I wrote my story. May you find joy in sharing your own.

Contents

Artwork by Bethany Schlegel Shaw

Introduction:
My Middle Name Used to be Joy

As a little girl, I hated my middle name "Joy." I was embarrassed by my silly parents and mumbled only my middle initial. When I got married, I pushed my joy aside and made my maiden name, Colbert, my middle name.

I hate to brag; shouting out about myself makes me very uncomfortable. As a shy girl, I learned that writing and sharing my experiences could boost my mood and keep me focused on the joy of my day. As I grew, I gained the courage to share because I wanted to remind people to look around and highlight the good that surrounds them.

This is my collection of stories that share a common thread; they all deliver bursts of joy. They are funny, sad, happy, and heartbreaking, but when I flip my pancake, I share the gooey joy that is trapped inside. I have included a toast since when asked to raise a glass at an event, you might be nervous and anxiously awaiting your turn. Whether it is a eulogy, birthday, graduation, bar mitzvah or wedding, sharing a good toast is stressful. Glasses clink, voices dim, and you are now the center of attention. You make your toast, and laughs twinkle around you, until the room breaks out in a firework of applause and "here, here's." You did it, you brought the room together in smiles and happy tears. That feeling is a joy burst.

> Think of all the joy you will find
> when you leave the world behind
> and bid your cares goodbye.
> Then you can FLY!
>
> Peter Pan,
> The Movie of Peter Pan

My father was the ultimate joy burster; always encouraging us to find things to look forward to, savor the moments of happiness around us, and remain hopeful. We would vacation with him each summer on Nantucket Island, where we soaked up time together as a family. We were not allowed to mention the weather, which almost always started off foggy on the island. We could not control it, so why waste energy on it? Rather, he taught us to focus on the rewards of our chores and the moments we were experiencing. "Does it get any better than this" would be his boisterous comment to the picturesque view, crashing waves, or the simple toast we were eating at breakfast.

My Dad had the ability to transform a warm piece of Portuguese bread into the most delicious meal with his descriptions. All of my complaints, arguments with my siblings, and worries would wash away once I sunk my teeth into the buttery toast. Going to the bakery to buy homemade Portuguese bread, cooking it to perfection for eggs, with cinnamon and sugar, or as the foundation for a beach sandwich, became our tradition. We shared this tradition with all of our house guests and it even had an honorable mention at my father's funeral. We raised our glasses to our father and his delicious buttery toast.

The best event toasts I have heard all start with a story about a memorable experience. Music hums in the background, laughter reaches across the table, and there is a spark of joy. A utensil taps on a glass, a voice rises and the chatter quiets as the room's attention shines on the speaker. The toast connects all who are gathered and they raise their glasses in unison to show their support. Sharing your own words of wisdom with an audience is the ultimate joy-recap.  My hope is that by telling my own tales, I will make readers laugh or cry, and inspire them to share a toast when they gather their own flocks.

The cover of my first book, self-published in 1983.

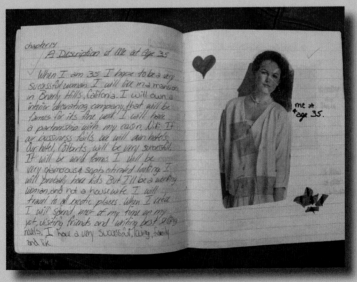

Earliest version of a goal-setting journal.

Act One: Celebrations

Little Mrs. Sunshine

"Your mother is going to be so surprised!" my father excitedly told Sarah and I as we were setting up the patio.

"I cannot wait to see her face," he exclaimed as he rushed around. "My secretary told me to put quarters in the freezer for when he gets started. And girls, please make sure my boombox isn't moved." It was the late 80s; an outdoor sound system did not exist.

The details our father explained did not make sense nor did we understand his plan. I drifted into my parent's room to check on my Mom. Dressed in a pastel floral sundress, hot rollers setting her hair, she was unaware of what the night had in store. My parents were on a wait list to get into Congressional Country Club near our home in Potomac, Maryland. In order to get accepted, they had to have numerous written recommendations from existing members. Their plan was to host a cocktail party for their friends who were members, and those friends would bring guests who belonged to the country club. They assumed that they would dazzle their guests, inspiring them to speak up on their behalf. The party happened to fall on my mother's fortieth birthday. Again, many of these guests were not her friends, but friends of friends belonging to the country club community.

Once the soiree was in full swing, I watched my Dad hop from cluster to cluster in his signature lemon and lime corduroy pants. My mom sashayed around the patio monitoring Sarah and me as we served cocktails. The crowd was stiff but the night was young.

I noticed one man looked a little out of place in the preppy crowd. His mullet hung over the collar of his tight Izod shirt, his muscular legs straining his shorts as he plugged in his boombox. Clearly not a fan of my Dad's cassette, he quickly switched the tape. My Mom offered to help him, giving me the hairy eyeball assuming I had over-served this guest. He suddenly pushed my mom into a chair, and the party came to a halt.

"Hot Thang, Barely Twenty-One," blasted from the boombox, and he swiftly tore off his shorts and began gyrating to the beat. As his clothes came off in rapid moves, my Dad laughed hysterically and we looked on with shock. The guests started pulling away from the stripping circle. My Dad was oblivious to their stares. "Girls, grab the quarters!" My sister and I looked at our mom with a sincere apology, noticing several guests leaving. But my mom, cool as ever, took it in stride. She was laughing and covering her face, shaking her head at my dad. Johnny O. finished his dance and posed for pictures for my Dad. He autographed his 8x10-glossy and strutted out of our life.

I think it goes without saying that my parents did not get accepted into the country club. We laugh to this day about my dad's terrible judgment. But true to his nature, he never seemed to regret hiring my mom a stripper for her birthday. As he always said, it turned out to be a good way to figure out they weren't cut out for that country club. Dad also succeeded in giving her what she really wanted—a big surprise for her birthday!

A few years later, my father brought Johnny O back to add to the fun of my cousin's birthday party. True form for my family to transform a mistake into a funny story. When my mother began dating twenty years later, we gave her boyfriend the nickname of Johnny O. and it stuck. We never forget a joke, and I can still sing all of the lyrics to his song.

Gramma Phyllis

Her crepe skin sagged over her jowls and rarely stretched into a smile. Only when she found double-chocolate Klondike bars or won a game of Pitch would she relax her Bitchy-Resting-Face. Phyllis walked into a room with her hands clenched in her pockets, waiting for an embrace that she would not reciprocate. Her signature outfits were a black and gold bathing suit in the summer and a gold lame blouse at Christmas. Both looks allowed her butterfly tattoo to peek out of her cleavage. We had her buried in her signature bathing suit.

Gramma Phyllis was not a warm and fuzzy grandmother. Instead of engaging in her negativity, I would focus on the glistening peaks of whipped cream peeking out of the cracks in the basket that accompanied her on each visit. Apple pie in the fall, lemon meringue in the spring, and blueberry in the summer. Gramma Phyllis's pies sweetened her snarky demeanor.

"My pool has been refreshing." *Translation*: you should come for a swim.

"I have been picking blueberries in my yard." *Translation*: if you come to visit, I will make your favorite blueberry pie.

"I always have Klondike bars in the freezer." *Translation*: you really should bring the kids.

Each year as a child, I would unhappily spend an overnight at my grandparent's house. I was scared of her brutal honesty, afraid of what she might say without my mom protecting me. After a night swim in her pool, I would get into my Holly Hobby pajamas and lay on her living room floor circling the toys I dreamed of owning in the Sears catalog. I would spend the evening circling Barbie accessories, Easy-Bake Ovens, and art supplies. Gramma would tell me stories of my mother's dolls, criticizing her for not taking good care of her possessions. Gramma did not buy me any gifts from the catalog, but she did encourage my dreaming.

When I was in kindergarten my mother's youngest brother was killed. My Uncle Chuckie was only eighteen when he skipped school with his buddy to play with a gun they found. The youngest of my mother's three brothers, his death left an enormous hole in my Gramma's heart. As my brother grew up, he looked like my uncle and Gramma would break down at holidays if she caught John in the right light. The tragedy changed my grandparent's relationship as each parent experienced their own waves of grief. They fought for gun safety in their town and Gramma used the settlement from the case to buy herself a swimming pool. She began each day with a swim, and I imagine it was her way of feeling closer to her baby boy.

When I was in college, my grandparents divorced, and Gramma Phyllis signified the occasion with a butterfly tattoo on her breast. I bragged to my sorority sisters that I had a cool grandmother with a tattoo.

Convertible top-down, smoke from her cigarette trailing behind her, Gramma Phyllis would pull into the driveway each holiday for an overnight visit. She would complain about the drive, bark at us to gather her things, and would dramatically drop her pie basket on the kitchen counter in a huff. My parents would not allow her to smoke indoors, so Gramma bought herself a LeBaron convertible and chain-smoked all the way to our house.

Each year Gramma Phyllis took a class to learn a new creative technique and gave us homemade Christmas gifts. She would stencil jewelry boxes, paint tote bags, and knit us cozy blankets. One year she made porcelain dolls that resembled my sister and me as little girls. While the dolls creep me out and live in my attic, I respect that she used her creative projects to demonstrate her love for us.

I did not appreciate getting a painted tray or wooden box as a teenager, but these are now my most treasured items displayed in our home. I entertain friends with her stenciled trays, carry my needlepoint in her tote bag, and her wooden swan decorates our living room. We use her picnic basket, plant succulents in her soup tureen, serve festive drinks in her punch bowl, and her domino collection is on display. These treasures help tell our story and keep her close to us. A reminder to encourage more making and creating in our own homes.

Once she settled in, we would gather around the table for an early Christmas Eve supper, and oohed and aahed as she lifted the warm meat pie out of Great Gramma Freeman's (her mother's) pie basket. A second dessert pie was underneath, typically chocolate cream unless she had frozen summer blueberries. Our friends would pop by after dinner, playing pool with my Dad. My mum and grandmother would slip out for the midnight Christmas Eve church service, an activity I did not understand. Both ladies fell asleep at nine o'clock most nights. Why would they choose to go out at 11:30 p.m.?

"The candlelight is beautiful and the music makes you cry," was the only explanation they gave. I would later learn it was the one time that they mourned the loss of Chuckie.

Gramma Phyllis's culinary talents were pies, devil dogs, and pancakes fried in butter to "get crispy edges." When she divorced my grandfather in her late 70s, Gramma had to increase her income. She lived in a small ranch home and could make the above treats well. She got creative and turned her home into a bed-n-breakfast, welcoming parents visiting their children at the nearby boarding school. Over the holidays, she added the sale of Christmas trees from the property behind her home.

Todd and I visited one December, bringing friends from Belmont to have an idyllic experience of cutting down our own Christmas tree. Very Norman Rockwell until we arrived for lunch and she offered us a can of soup to share among the four of us and handed us each an invoice for a $10 tree purchase. After our soup, we went into the field behind her house and we cut down scraggly Charlie Brown Christmas trees. Gramma was on a tight budget. She only treated herself to Klondike bars and an annual trip to Hampton Beach with her "Ya-Ya Sisters." But she did start and end each day with a swim in the pool she bought herself (the night swim often in her birthday suit).

Gramma loved to smoke and slather her leather skin in tanning oil. Two habits that didn't help her longevity. A persistent cough led to the diagnosis at eighty-one that she had lung cancer. After watching her daughter (aka my mother) and son-in-law (my father) fight through chemo treatments, Gramma decided to let nature take its course. Sarah and I drove down to say goodbye and she got mad when Sarah began to cry. Gramma was not a woman who allowed any time for self-pity. We returned to her bedside when she slipped into a coma and painted her toenails. It was important to us that her pedicure match her bathing suit so she could dive right into heaven.

Here's the thing about my Gramma Phyllis, in life, she was a prickly pear, and our interactions were abrasive. We learned to share our creative gifts together, creating traditions to pass along the way. As I aged, I realized that the seeds she planted were meant to help me grow. From her, I learned to be brave and strong in the worst of times. It took time, but she stood up for herself and spent her last chapter doing what she wanted. Sunbathing by her pool, reading romance novels, and eating ice cream. I celebrate her birthday each year by doing something brave.

STICK UP FOR
YOURSELF AND
BRAVELY FOLLOW
YOUR HEART
CHEERS!

The Wedding Invite

"Please ask Mary to send Gramma a new invitation," my mother requested. "You addressed her invite to Gramma Phyllis and she did not want her mailman to know that she is a grandmother." WTF, isn't she proud to be my grandmother? Isn't she excited about my wedding? I was too annoyed and embarrassed to ask Mary, my mother-in-law, to send my grandmother an invite without her title.

At our wedding I introduced her to one of my college friends; John McLean. Gramma was anxious about being a new divorcee at our wedding and not having anyone to dance with. John McLean is our friend who can make anyone he talks to feel as if they are the most important person in the room. John asks very detailed questions and laughs with a sparkle in his eye that dazzles anyone in his presence. When Todd and I meet someone new, we try to pepper them with questions and listen intently to their answers. We call this "pulling a John McLean."

Introducing John to Gramma was the best move I made that evening. They danced and he spun her around the makeshift dance floor and I watched Gramma tossing her head back with laughter as he twirled her about.

"I have shirts older than you," she flirted.

And just like that, Gramma forgot about anyone knowing that she was my grandmother.

Do one thing
every day that
scares you.

~Eleanor Roosevelt

Butterfly Tat

"I finally stood up for myself," Gramma explained as she announced her separation from Grandpa Joe. I wasn't sure what that really meant, but Gramma cracked a smile; a rare occurrence.

She began her days with a swim, got a job at a local jewelry store, and joined the *Red Hat Club*. She followed a strict budget and learned how to master a fried hot dog for her dinner-for-one. Topped off with a Klondike bar and a skinny dip in her pool, and she was content. She was confident that she was teaching Joe a lesson.

Meanwhile, Grandpa Joe did not know how to do his laundry so he brought his clothes to a dry cleaner. He shared his tragic story and the owner, a big-bosomed soul who invited him to stay with her. This was not part of Gramma's plan.

They proceeded with a divorce, both too stubborn to admit they were wrong. Her head held high, Gramma went to a tattoo parlor and had a butterfly tattooed on her left breast. She told me that she was free to fly and she peeled back her signature gold lame blouse to show me the wings of the butterfly peeking out of her lacy bra.

The following year, they began dating each other. On one visit to my home for Christmas Gramma quickly explained, "we will be sharing a bed on this visit." No further explanation was needed, and no comment from Grandpa Joe who followed her with his bag. She had gotten a license to transform her house into a bed-n-breakfast, giving her additional income and company. She ended her nights with a skinny dip and then would invite Grandpa Joe over on her terms.

She figured it out in her last chapter. She spread her wings and became the beautiful butterfly she was always meant to be.

THERE IS NOTHING BETTER
THAN FEELING
IMPORTANT.

HERE'S TO
HELPING
OTHERS SHINE!

RAISE YOUR GLASS

The Last Easter Egg

As soon as we transformed our eleven year friendship into a romance, I wanted to have children with Todd. We were married young and it was four years before we started to plan. This was the year my father's cancer took a turn and with grief, often comes gratitude for the ones we love. At twenty-nine I learned early how short life was going to be.

We had been married for four years when a firework burst inside me sending us a dramatic sign that it was time.

"I have sharp gas pains in my side and need to go home," I blushed to my boss Amanda. I leaned into the cramp as she called an ambulance. AMBULANCE, C'MON? This was humiliating. I needed to simply leave and toot my way out the door. Amanda did not give me a choice so I kindly asked her not to bother Todd at work. As my ambulance pulled into Boston's Mass General Hospital, Todd opened the door to my ride. So much for secrecy. As he pushed me down the corridor in a wheelchair, we heard "Paging Todd Colbert, there is a call for TODD COLBERT" over the loudspeaker. That had my anxious mother written all over it since who else would combine my maiden name with Todd? Quickly after being admitted, both Todd's sister and my father arrived to check on me, sneaking peanut M&Ms to Todd behind my head. An ultrasound revealed a burst ovarian cyst and I was scheduled for laparoscopic surgery.

A week prior, we had gone horseback riding in Jackson Hole on my Dad's Bucket List adventure. It was assumed that I had jostled the cyst and there were probably others waiting to explode. I woke from surgery to Todd and my parents with matching goofy grins on their faces. "Time to get you pregnant per the doctor's orders," Todd explained. He had removed severe endometriosis, but it would grow back again. While my periods had been horribly painful, I had always assumed that was what everyone else felt. Once again I regretted not gathering feedback from other women on what they were experiencing.

We went away with our childhood friends to the Dominican Republic and I came back with Tyler on board. As soon as we conceived, my doctor reminded me that I should try and get pregnant immediately after giving birth if we wanted more children. I had no idea how difficult that would be.

Todd dared me to keep my first pregnancy a secret until I was twelve weeks along. I am not known to be a good secret keeper, but I took on this challenge. Easter landed right at this time and we invited both of our families over to celebrate. We hid plastic candy-filled eggs in the yard of our new home and included the "golden egg" which shared the news of my pregnancy.

My Dad arrived with my sister Natalie in a Porsche he borrowed from a colleague. I think that he wanted to feel the wind in his greying hair. I think he was feeling a little aged and wanted to feel the wind in his hair. *Father-of-the-Bride* was also our favorite movie so he might have been mimicking Steve Martin in the sequel.

The "golden egg" was a tradition that my father-in-law passed down from Todd's grandfather. Our niece and nephew went out on the hunt and quickly recovered the prized egg. I revealed my T-shirt which displayed a cartoon baby *in utero*. After having endometriosis surgery earlier that year, we had a lot to celebrate with this pregnancy.

It's a joke in my family that I love Easter because I am a jelly bean and peep addict, and my great grandmother's ambrosia is my favorite dish to make. But truly I love remembering that golden egg and the celebration with both parents. A sweet memory I will cherish forever.

Baking Babies

As soon as Tyler arrived, I was told that we should try to get pregnant quickly before my endometriosis grows back. This time was not as easy. Eighteen months of infertility drugs to speed up nature while adding crazy hormones to my already chaotic mind, I graduated to IVF. The first round didn't work and if I wasn't feeling like a failure before, this sealed the deal. They were mixing our batter and sliding the cake into my oven, but the souffle would fall and I would receive the call that we could not bake a baby.

I went to an acupuncturist who built a mini-fire pit around my belly button, crisscrossing little X's to my button O. As she inserted teeny needles, she explained that she was sending all the warmth to my uterus to prepare for conception. We decided to try IVF one last time and as we were packing to go to celebrate the Fourth of July on Nantucket, I get the call that my eggs were ready. I never wanted to disrupt the fun, so I got permission to pack the medications on ice and asked my mother and Aunt Judi to help me administer them. Having nurses in the family paid off.

My father and his brother were called "Irish Twins" since they were born ten months apart. Uncle Fred and Aunt Judi were second parents to me and the majority of my childhood memories involve them and my cousins. The family gathered for a traditional Fourth of July barbeque, Stoli raspberry cocktails, and while my young toddler chased sparklers dressed in his red, white and blue outfit from Old Navy, I cried.

They convinced me to call the clinic and push my retrieval back a day so we did not have to ferry off the island and miss any of the celebration. *I will not be the reason we are sitting in the dreaded Cape-Cod-traffic*, I thought to myself. It may sound like I did not really want to get pregnant, but at this point in my infertility journey, I was deflated. I also never give more than eighty percent.

In everything I do I come out of the gates fast but slow down by the finish. Maybe this was not what nature intended and I was tempting fate, I wondered. The clinic had reminded me that our chances were slim. It was easier to protect myself by not getting my hopes up. I took this as a sign to soak up the sunshine with my family. Aunt Judi pulled me into the bathroom and she and my mother stabbed my butt cheek with needles. We all tossed back our Stoli's and wished for the best.

I could not bear hearing bad news again and asked Todd to be the contact for the clinic. The best burst of Fourth of July fireworks came from the call Todd received with the miraculous news that I was pregnant with Mason.

We gave Tyler a baby doll who he named "Baby Pete." Baby Pete helped us to practice adding a new little person to our trio. When Mason Robert arrived that Spring, we knew he would set the world on fire.

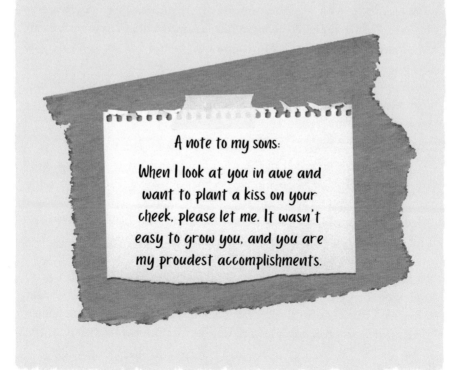

A note to my sons:

When I look at you in awe and want to plant a kiss on your cheek, please let me. It wasn't easy to grow you, and you are my proudest accomplishments.

Pookie and the Pea

"We aren't sure if we will be able to make it to your graduation."

Deep in my college bubble, I didn't hear much on the phone conversation after that. My baby sister was almost two and my Mom had not had a mammogram since before she was pregnant. She went on to explain that she had found a hard pea in her breast and was now diagnosed with stage four breast cancer, two weeks before my college graduation. Her mastectomy was scheduled and my family flew down to North Carolina for the ceremony. I was anxious about heading out into the real world and this news was over-whelming. My parents were a young, happy couple with four children and a new home in Wellesley, Massachusetts. We did not have any family history of illness and I still had all of my grandparents alive.

That summer, my sister Sarah and I took care of Natalie while our mom went through an intense chemo-treatment plan. I moved to D.C. that fall, and traveled home frequently. Less than two years later, my father was diagnosed with prostate cancer at forty-nine, a rare occurrence at his age. Feeling the guilt of my mom just recovering, I moved back to Massachusetts when my Dad began his treatment. I had gone to school in the south to relocate to warmer weather, but cancer made this seem selfish. As the oldest, it didn't seem fair to my siblings to live so far away. Todd had also relocated to Washington, D.C. from Massachusetts and then cancer changed our plans.

A second pea appeared in the scar of my Mom's mastectomy, almost twenty years after the first debut. The chance of having cancer twice in the same spot is rare, but cancer is persistent. This time was worse since Pookie lived alone, but our muscle memory was strong. She kicked cancer's ass, and when he came back, she let him know he was not welcome. After losing my father to cancer, we became chemo experts. We knew how to be helpful, but as a young mom, my own energy was depleted. I drew and wrote many stories about the "Adventures of Pookie and the Cancer Monster." Focusing on the funny moments of each day was extremely therapeutic and gave me a medium to share the experience with our little boys.

When chemo destroyed her heart valve and she needed to have open-heart surgery, we dressed her up in funny wigs and wrote songs about her bald head.

Cancer is finally not with us anymore, and at each celebration, we toast to being healthy. We do not live in fear of when he is coming back, but savor the days he is not at the table. We use all of these experiences to help those living with cancer in their lives. We do not allow the peas to cause any more discomfort in our life.

Feed your brain;
she is a sponge
and if you point
her toward the sky,
she will absorb the sun,
the moon,
and all of the stars.
CHEERS!

Good Morning Campers!

My Gramma Phyllis secretly saved money to send my mother to summer camp. Attending camp opened my mother's eyes to a wilder world, teaching her independence and giving her a break from the endless chores of living on a farm.

I went to overnight camp once, but two days in, I got my period for the first time. Shy and nervous, I could barely explain my situation to the camp nurse. Armed with a box of pads, I wrote letters about my misery to my Mum from my top bunk. Too shy to speak up, I washed my Wonder Woman undies behind our cabin and counted the days until it was time to go home.

When we began researching camps for our sons, I was amazed to learn that my camp had a great reputation and we knew many friends sending their children. I told our boys a less bloody version of why I didn't enjoy camp, re-framing my memories in a positive light. I highlighted the talent show, horseback riding and campfire stories. It is really about mind games. If you can switch a negative thought or memory into a positive one, you can train yourself to be happier. It is okay to have negative thoughts, they just should be balanced with good ones so they do not overwhelm your brain.

The first summer Tyler went, I waited ten long days to hear from him. One of the rules of the camp is that they don't bring any electronics, and parents cannot email their children. This allows them to fully engage and decreases their chances of being homesick. Our family dynamic shifted with having one son at home, and I learned to adjust. We got one postcard on day ten, which I re-read a dozen times analyzing if he seemed happy by his use of exclamation points.

When we picked him up, Tyler could not contain his excitement as he shared his adventures and toured us around the campground. He returned the following summer with his brother, and they shared a few sessions together. While they learned a lot during the experience, it also shaped all of our futures.

You can find lots of articles on why camp is a great experience for the child, but it should also be a recommendation from marriage therapists. Some years we went on mini-vacations, other times we enjoyed stay-cations.

Being without the kids did remind us why we started this journey in the first place. We didn't fight over parenting issues. We didn't discuss the kids very much, since we really didn't have much to discuss. The camp they went to did not allow electronics, and since they aren't great letter writers, a postcard on day 10 doesn't give you a lot of material. We slept naked, shopped for dinner at the store each evening like we were French, and we watched inappropriate TV shows while we ate dinner on the coffee table at 6 pm.

"Good morning campers," is my mother's signature greeting, and the way she starts each toast, a legacy in itself.

What I learned during the two weeks we sent our boys to summer camp:

* I am a creative, thoughtful, and calm person when not caught in the blender of parenting.

* Even though I get my energy from people, I do enjoy the quiet house.

* Grocery shopping is not a chore when you pop into the market to select items for one or two meals. Basically, pretending I am French.

* Sleeping naked is enjoyable and decreases night sweats. It is hard to do this when the boys are home.

* Sex cures a lot of issues.

* You can take trips as a couple, but being home together and navigating real life can also be a treat. Eating take-out on your coffee table while watching inappropriate TV brings you back to the early days.

* It is nice to realize that our arguments stem from parenting and that we can still connect as a couple. This reminder always helped us stay on course for the year before they went back to camp.

* Having camp on your calendar will give your family something to look forward to during a time when the future is bleak. We often gave camp sweatshirts, trunks, lanterns, sleeping bags, and other items at Christmas to build excitement for the upcoming summer.

CAPTURE AS MUCH
AS YOU CAN WITH
YOUR OWN HERD.

YOU NEVER KNOW
WHICH FRIENDS
MIGHT APPEAR
LATER IN YOUR NEST.

CHEERS!

For the Love
of Breakdancing

Love often catches us by surprise. There are tons of cliches: it comes in many forms, it ensures all things, and it is also a battlefield. I believe it all except the fact that you can look for it in all the wrong places.

I met Todd in the sixth-grade homeroom. His laugh was contagious, his flirty spirit sweet, but his breakdance moves in his cute parachute pants were out of this world. We were thirteen when I first saw him, a folded piece of cardboard under his arm as he strutted out to recess in his zipper-adorned parachute pants. His buddy Pete followed behind him with the boombox, a mixed cassette tape in his back pocket. We girls hung close enough to watch but far enough to appear deep in a conversation. I only had the courage to talk to Todd in the comfort of our seats in Homeroom. Our friends Brad, Ed, Jason, Sue, Paolo, and Pete were in between us, fated to sit together by our last names which sealed the deal on our life-long friendship. I was at the head of the row as a Colbert, Todd picked up the rear. He was inches shorter than me, we had matching braces, and we became fast friends.

Like a top, Todd spun on his head, parachute pants blowing in the wind, and my tween heart skipped a beat. Our friendship grew during recess in middle school until our family moved to Maryland for my father's work. My family moved mid-semester of our eighth-grade year so I could make friends before the summer. Or that is what my parents told me when they broke the terrible news that we were moving from the only home I knew. My Dad bought a computer with a printer (this must be a big promotion for him I thought) and I typed letters to Todd.

We didn't make long-distance phone calls in the 80s. I picked up a pen and went in search of an audience for my complaints. Todd won the prize and we became pen pals. Little did he know, he would take on this role for life. We wrote until Todd caught me sending the same letter to all of our friends in Belmont. From that point on, I had to handwrite his letters planning my annual visit to Massachusetts.

In one exchange, Todd told me about the *Chenery Middle School Eighth Grade Dance.* I guilted my parents into flying me north and Todd asked his breakdancing buddy John to ask me as his date. I permed my hair, my Mom bought me the pink lace dress with matching fingerless gloves that I selected, and I provided the stack of rubber bracelets. She insisted on sewing ribbon straps to my dress which altered the *Madonna-Like-A-Virgin* look I was going for, but I tied a bow in my hair and hoped for the best. I danced with Todd strictly as a time to catch up on our respective evenings.

As soon as I graduated, my parents relocated back to Massachusetts and I would reconnect with Todd in person. We would share pizza and discuss our crushes, current hopes, and dreams. When he got his first job as a merchant marine and sailed off on a ship to Chile, we became pen pals again. Our friendship grew with the invention of email. That sound of the email dialing up can bring me right back to listening to R.E.M. in my Virginia apartment, reading about his adventures on the Panama Canal. When Todd pulled into the dock, we would visit on the shore and laugh over the stories we told each other via snail mail.

Todd was a firecracker whose smile lit up the room and flirty quick wit made him fun for my whole family. My parents would hire him to bartend their parties, Sarah would ask him to chauffeur her to prom, and he didn't blink an eye when my Dad suggested that they paint the house together for our wedding reception. Almost forty years later, these qualities make him a great husband and father. His dance moves in middle school were magical, but today those only emerge when we get invited to a wedding.

The next time we would dance would be at our friend Sue's wedding a decade later. Todd and the gang stayed at my apartment in Virginia and we all went to the first wedding of one of our own. We teased and flirted and at one point, kissed on the ballroom balcony. We did not speak of this drunken kiss and Todd shipped out in the merchant marine.

For weeks, I would find notes hidden under my pillow, in my drawers, and in various spots in our apartment. No one else could make me laugh with a post-it note. We wrote letters and laughed over the crazy kiss that had to have happened as we were swept up in the romance attending our first wedding.

After a summer to save after graduation, I moved with my friends Loren and Casey to Virginia. Todd got off his three-month cruise to Alaska and I convinced him to relocate to Virginia.

"We are looking for a fourth roommate, it's a no-brainer," I urged.

His version involves me asking him to sign a lease, but we agree to disagree. He needed a buoy to lift his damp spirits. We didn't have cell phones, so communication wasn't what it is today.

And that's how it came to be that he drove ten hours without stopping, arriving at our townhouse with his childhood dresser hanging out of the trunk of his Jetta. He parked next to my friend Sue's care who we had just given the fourth bedroom to. At the time, it seemed logical to share my bed platonically with my childhood friend.

After going to the Samples concert, we were talking about a girl he wanted to ask out on a date. I couldn't stop criticizing her clothing. We were still buzzing from the concert but this new feeling of jealousy was something entirely confusing. Todd's eyes lit up and he leaned in and kissed me in our kitchen, over a tub of ice cream. I expected his kiss to be sweet, slow, and lingering. I was blown away by the explosion of fireworks that I felt. How could I feel this way for Todd Greenfield?

Our relationship changed and Todd taught me to have spontaneous fun. We would play pool at a local dive bar, bike around the Washington Monument, or catch part of a tour in one of the many free museums. He would steal kisses from me in the aisle of a store, walking the city streets, or whenever we were alone. To this day, Todd jumps right in, enjoys the moment, and wears his heart on his sleeve.

Right Under My Nose

I called home from a payphone in my college dorm.

"Sorry honey, we can't talk right now. We are in the middle of a party for your Dad."

Thanks for the invite, I muttered under my breath. My parents only believed in flying me home from school at Christmas and summer break. In addition to the 50th birthday party of my Dad's, I missed my cousin's wedding, but thankfully it wasn't her last.

"Oh, my! Todd has your Uncle Fred in a fit of laughter, gotta hang up!" my mother sang into the phone.

"Excuse me, did you say Todd?"

"Yes, Sami, we hired Todd Greenfield to bartend," she replied, annoyed that I did not comprehend. "It's Sarah's cotillion dance and he drove her and her cute date Brad before the party started."

It seemed Todd was more a part of our family than I was. I could hear his distinct laugh in the background making me homesick.

I flew home two weeks later for Christmas. I sat at the kitchen counter and confessed to my mother that I was breaking up with my southern boyfriend. He was asleep in the guest room, having come to visit me before I was leaving for a winter term in London.

I expected my mother to be disappointed since my parents hated hosting any boyfriends. To my surprise, she wasn't the least bit shocked.

"Well, he's no Todd Greenfield," my mother exclaimed as I cried.

"What does TODD Greenfield have to do with anything?" I asked.

The reference to my pal Todd gave me pause. Todd was the big brother I never had. Todd with the mischievous grin and flirty nature? TODD, I questioned?

"C'mon Sami, don't you have feelings for your Todd? He is really wonderful," my Mom crooned.

NOPE, this was a crazy idea. But it also stayed with me on my trip to London, during my last semester of college, and when I moved back home after graduation.

It was three years before we started dating, but as a mother now, I often wonder if my Mum could see something before me? It often takes someone to point something or someone out to you who is right under your nose.

> Taking the time to recap
> will allow you to
> appreciate what is
> right in front of you!

Did You Really Give Me a Cookbook?

We had been secretly together for a few months but we were not sure how to label our relationship. *When Harry Met Sally* was my favorite movie and I was afraid we would ruin our friendship if we started dating. Todd had been my closest friend since we moved from Belmont in eighth grade. All throughout high school and college, I'd told Todd everything. Every crush I had, all of my insecurities, my dreams, and fears, I confided in Todd. I had ruined my share of male friendships by getting romantically involved and I did not want to lose this one.

Todd and I were living in Northern Virginia and my roommates knew the details of our scandalous affair and our "no emotions" agreement. It all seemed manageable until we came home to Massachusetts for Christmas. Could we act platonic around our friends and family? Should we give each other gifts? If I didn't give him a gift and he gave me one, would I look like a jerk? Yet if I gave him a gift and he did not have one for me, would he think I had deeper feelings for him? The situation was stressful! Todd had recently moved into a house with my friend Rob. Never having lived on his own before, Todd was learning how to cook. A cookbook seemed like the perfect gift to give—one that would not send the wrong message.

My parents were hosting a Christmas Party, and Todd stopped by. We flirted all night and when he went to leave, he asked, "So you don't have a present for me?" I flushed and admitted that I had a gift for him but had forgotten to give it.

"Oh Sami, I thought we agreed to just be friends? But you bought me a present?"

I stammered with embarrassment, "It's not a Christmas present. I thought you could use a cookbook, and since you were nice to pick me up from the airport, I wanted to give you something." I was ten shades of red and mortified that I had admitted having feelings.

"Ok, just to confirm that you did not buy me a PRESENT," he said with a twinkle in his eye.

I gave him the cookbook, continuing to downplay my gift. As Todd got his coat on to leave, he leaned in and kissed me on the cheek.

"Merry Christmas Sami. That big box under the tree is my present to you."

I ran over to my parent's Christmas tree and opened a big white box that contained blue corduroy overalls, with a white blouse. An outfit I had admired when we had gone to the mall a month earlier.

"I can't wait to see you in this outfit. Merry Christmas." Once again, Todd's surprise blew me away.

I recently found the cookbook that I gave him and my inscription suggesting that we make a blueberry pie. I must not have had Gramma Phyllis's recipe since no one could compete with her pies. We started cooking dinners together, adding cookbooks to our collection as the years went on. When Todd and I visit our friend's homes, we like to give them cookbooks to promise future gatherings and inspire them to try new recipes. Truly a gift that keeps on giving.

And Then God Sent Us Todd

The weekend we got engaged, my mother-in-law baked a cake and hosted my family for a backyard barbeque celebration. Both of my parents were in their late forties and had battled cancer, so we were also celebrating their dual remissions.

We raised our glasses and my mother, "Pookie," read her toast, connecting our families and kicking off our engagement year. Pookie is not someone who gets up at an event and speaks to a crowd. My mother has had the supporting role for most of my life, even after her co-star died, she did not step into his spotlight. As I look at the framed version of the toast she gave at our engagement, I think about how out of her comfort zone this act was. To date, the only times I've ever seen my mother speak in front of a crowd was at my engagement party and my sister Sarah's wedding.

You can learn a lot from a toast. The giver often shares background stories of what you are celebrating. In the case of my mom, she explained how Todd and I got together after eleven years of friendship. Both of my parents were in remission from cancer and my Mom credited fate and God as what brought Todd and the Greenfields into their lives.

After the death of my father, my mother knew she'd eventually have to sell our happy place; the home where we'd grown up. She warned us for a decade, but it still came as a surprise when she finally did it. Every year since my father died eighteen years before, we discussed her desire to sell the home they had planned to retire in. It never actually moved beyond the emotional conversation, until the pandemic, and real estate prices sky-rocketed to heights the area hadn't seen before. It took just a week for another family to see its potential and grab it, ready to make their own memories. I can't even think about them enjoying that incredible view, those bright stars, and that ocean breeze that instantly turned my hair into wool. Losing Wanoma Way has been a tough loss to recover from.

We spent the Fourth of July holiday in a new spot. We swapped burgers for southern barbeque, bagels for biscuits, and explored South Carolina. We broke a tradition of running a road race with family and friends and opted instead for jet skis and hush puppies. We were lucky to be invited to friends' homes for additional weekend getaways, and both our sons worked at country clubs, saving their summer earnings to enjoy during the school year.

Todd channeled his energy into our own home. He planted new flowers, removed trees that blocked our sunshine, fertilized our lawn, and gave our house a fresh face lift with new paint and lighting. I worked on our herb garden, cooked new meals, and replaced our porch with furnishing to encourage gathering for endless conversations. I napped, read, and enjoyed a glass of wine like I was away on that magical island. In the midst of our grief, our home received more of our love and attention.

While I miss that house by the sea, our own home has been like a warm hug, and I feel good returning to her. Leave it to Todd to weave in productive projects while shifting my attention to what we have, versus what we have lost. My Mom was right when she gave the toast at our engagement: "And Then God Sent Us Todd."

Thank God for sending us Todd.

Marry Me

My Dad met Todd at the golf course, but he put a wrench in Todd's plan by bringing my sister Natalie along for the ride. The diamond engagement ring was burning a hole in his backpack. Todd went to my parent's home to ask for his blessing, but my father changed plans and was not home. Todd wanted to ask the question in person and now he had to get creative.

My father and I had plans to run Boston's Corporate Challenge 5K road race which we completed annually. My father wasn't feeling up for a run, so he opted to walk with a few co-workers. Todd stood on the street corner of the Ritz-Carlton Hotel where he worked as an engineer, scanning the moving crowd in search of my father. As soon as he spotted him, Todd yelled across Newbury Street, "Hey Jack, I have an important question to ask you!" My father laughed and waved but did not stop. Don't you want to go see what he wants" asked his curious co-worker. "Oh, Todd is always joking," my Dad explained.

"C'mon Jack, I NEED to talk to you!" Seeing that he was losing his opportunity, Todd yelled as loud as he could, "JACK, I want to ask Sami to marry me tomorrow! Do I have your blessing?"

"That sounds pretty serious?" asked the co-worker, and my clueless Dad just laughed, still believing that Todd was pulling his leg.

My father knew I was heading to the Red Hat, a bar on Beacon Hill after the race. He showed up at the bar, came back to my table, met everyone, and then whispered to me, "I saw Todd." He stopped mid-sentence and quickly explained that he had to head home. The whole interaction was bizarre, but I went on with my evening.

As my father drove home, he called his brother to ask for his perspective. He had my Aunt Judi on the line as well and called his sister after the call to get her opinion. Once he arrived home, he shared the details of the entire evening with my Mom. Everyone had the same message to him: call Todd. Together my parents called Todd, who was not happy to hear that so many members of the Colbert family knew about his secret plans to propose.

Later that night, I told Todd about seeing my Dad and he contained his frustration.

"Are you going for a run tomorrow?" Todd asked as we got into bed.

"No, I'm going to take tomorrow off," I replied.

"C'mon, I made you a new mix tape," he pleaded. We went back and forth and I thought it was odd that Todd was pushing me to run, but I agreed since he seemed very proud of his mix tape creation.

Early the next morning, I rode the subway into Boston, my Ann Taylor suit on a hanger over my shoulder. I left my things in a locker at FitCorp and ran down Beacon Street, enjoying the city as it was waking up. Once I crossed over the pink Arthur Fiedler footbridge, Todd's recorded voice boomed into my ears. He told me how much he loved me and how grateful he was that our friendship transformed into a relationship. I thought it was a sweet way of telling me that I was "the one," but that it was going to be a little while until he proposed. An "I love you but cannot afford a diamond ring" mix tape.

We both loved Neil Diamond, and his new album began playing into my yellow Sony Walkman. The song "Marry Me" started as I ran along the Charles River, passing the Hatch Shell. As I ran across the footbridge, a pink golf ball rolled across my path, and I stopped to pick it up. Todd rolled out from behind the bushes on rollerblades and got down on one knee. I enthusiastically chattered about how surprised I was to see him as he balanced on his knee, holding a ring box. I enthusiastically said yes to his proposal.

Later that day, Dad came to our apartment with a dozen golf balls and a dozen roses to apologize for making things so complicated. We danced to the song Marry Me at our wedding, and the lyrics are framed on our bedroom wall. The golf ball currently sits on my dresser, and twenty-six years later, it is a beautiful reminder of that incredible proposal. The cassette tape is long gone, but how I wish I could play it today. As far as proposals go, Todd's was sheer perfection.

Our marriage has taught me that words matter. I love you, my pleasure, and a simple thank you can go a long way. At our wedding reception, my father invited guests to return the following morning for a recap brunch. When he said, "If you are still in the yard and can't find your way out of the tent," he set the tone. This would be a night to remember.

Everybody Hurts, Sometimes

I thought if I went as his date to the wedding, we would have such a magical time that he would fall into deep-like. My dating strategy followed the script of a rom-com, but they never had the happily ever after ending. I flew home to Boston with the sad reality that this boy just wanted a date to a wedding, nothing more.

I wasn't saying very much on the drive home from the airport. Todd had picked me up and came back the following day when I called him in distress. As we sat in the hard waiting room chairs, Todd held my hand and listened to the vet drone on. Blah, blah, blah, kidney failure, blah, blah, cancer, blah, cats don't really have nine lives. Todd didn't let go when I called my parents, interrupting their cocktail party on Nantucket to deliver the news that I was killing the family cat Snuggles.

I cried in the front seat of his grandfather's car, the empty cat carrier rattling in the backseat. At twenty-five, my life seemed miserable. I was unlucky in love, my mom had aggressive breast cancer, my baby sister had special needs, and I was unemployed.

Todd slipped his favorite cassette into the car's tape deck. REM crooned "Everybody hurts" into the car.

"Did you even like that cat?" Todd asked.

"No, he scared me."

"Isn't your mom celebrating her break in chemo which is good news?

And does this guy even deserve you?"

"Yes she is and no he is nothing special," I whimpered.

"Aren't you moving to DC with Loren and Casey in the fall? Sounds like a lot of fun to me."

By my side when I was sad, but always re-framing to find the joy peeking inside of my misery. Todd was never afraid to tell me honestly how he felt and shed a different light on things for me.

"He doesn't sound that into you. Time to move on," he coached numerous times. A girlfriend would never be that direct. For eleven years we were friends and this kind of honesty was what I appreciated about our friendship.

Twenty-five years later, I want him to sugarcoat messages, let me down easy, and mince words. We argue when he is so honest, but I am realizing I need to remember that this style is what I cherished about being his friend.

When we saw a marriage therapist, the first thing she did was ask us to write about how we met, fell in love, and what attracted us to each other in the beginning. I found this exercise to be frustrating since I wanted to dive into the issues and work together on immediate solutions. Todd diligently did his homework and crafted touching answers to her questions. We were stuck in the weeds of parenting, and she helped us clear a path back to where we started.

It may hurt sometimes, but Todd tells it like it is and that kind of relationship is very special. I am also not beyond asking for someone else to help remind me of what is right in front of my face.

CHOOSE YOUR WORDS WISELY AND NEVER UNDERESTIMATE THEIR IMPACT.

RAISE YOUR GLASS

Apologies In Disguise

1. Read before you go to sleep. It's important to end your day without worries swirling around in your head.

2. Say you are sorry when you're wrong.

These are just two of the rules that I push in our home. They work for me. I feel better if I read at night because I worry a lot and want a good night's sleep. Growing up, my mom pushed "never go to bed angry," but a therapist helped me to realize that rule is not helpful. Often we need to have space before we can discuss the issue at hand.

A friend recently called me upset that her husband wouldn't apologize. She told me the story which sounded like many of my arguments with Todd.

"And now he wants me to go to dinner with him! I am too angry to do that! Until he apologizes, I am ignoring him," she complained.

"Go to dinner. That could be his apology in a costume." I suggested.

"Fine, I guess," she agreed. She called me the next morning gushing over their nice date night.

Two weeks later I went to bed frustrated over a comment Todd made. The next morning when he acted as if nothing happened, I was annoyed. We went about our day cleaning the garage, working in the yard, and completing general house chores. My anger festered. Todd went out to do errands and returned with flowers. I remember the advice I recently gave my friend. I accepted the flowers as an apology in disguise.

True Love

"Ugggh, I've lost my AirPods in the snow, and I have been looking as hard as you would, I swear" I whined into the phone to Todd.

"I am giving up, I need to get back to work!' I stomped around Wellesley Center, one lonely AirPod in my mitten, searching the sidewalk again for a white AirPod in the snow, making a needle in a haystack seem easy.

One woman stopped to ask me what I lost and snarked about why she only buys headphones on cords. Not helpful advice at the time.

I shuffled back to my office wondering what I should do with my lone pod.

An hour later my phone lit up with a text from Todd and a photo of the other pair riding shotgun in his car. "How did you find it?" I squealed with delight! I was not too surprised since Todd has an impressive level of persistence.

"I was on my hands and knees sifting through the snow (ok, I didn't even bend down to search) when an older woman stopped next to me. She asked if I was making a snowman and laughed at her joke but then began to pray to St. Anthony, the patron saint of lost things. And voila, we both spotted your AirPod shining up at us in a bed of snowflakes!"

I did not ask Todd to drive by the scene of the crime. I didn't have to. He knew how upset I was and solved the problem for me in a flash. True love in its finest form.

Here is to learning about love as we age, planting seeds, making memories, and sharing your neighborhood with your loved ones.

It is not easy, but if you can savor the good moments, and find a way to let the bad times work in our favor, our love will age like a fine wine (or at least something that will get you buzzed).

RAISE YOUR GLASS

Beaks up, wings out, it's time to celebrate you!

Hey birthday baby! A few things to remember before you blow out those candles:

In 2021, I had a milestone birthday and let everyone around me know how much I enjoy celebrating and making wishes. There was a lot of time for self-reflection this year and I was not alone in my hopes for positive changes for the future. As you know, I love a good recap, so here are my top lessons learned in my 49th year, to inspire you when you blow out your own candles.

1. Get moving first thing in the morning. Doing something for yourself is a great way to start the day.

2. Send an abundance of thank you texts, cards, and calls. You can never over-thank people.

3. Doing something good makes you feel good. "Helper's High" or "Giver's Glow" appear when we're contributing to the community around us.

4. Be a curious little monkey.

5. Toss your shell, share your inner core, and watch your nerd herd rally around you. It can be an idea, something you read or saw that brought you joy or a funny picture of yourself, but you never know who benefits from a boost.

6. Prep time is key. Batch food prep cooking on Sunday, ironing outfits to eliminate decision fatigue, laying out exercise clothes on the floor next to your bed. Plan your adult Garanimals: I have bought the same pants in two colors to make getting dressed easier.

7. Say yes to new adventures and worry about logistics AFTER the commitment. Have faith that it will work out.

8. Channel Mr. Rogers and change into slippers for virtual meetings. I like to add earrings as well for my own flair.

9. Never underestimate the power of a good night's sleep.

10. Send it: a quick text, a photo, a funny meme. It doesn't take a lot of time to brighten someone else's day.

11. Map it: create a vision of your hopes, dreams, and plans to see your future and chase it.

12. Lean on others' strengths. Phone a friend for a different perspective.

13. Share what you enjoy without concern over what people think. We built an owl nest and I posted it on social media because it made me smile. Turns out, it made a lot of other people smile too. I could not have predicted that by creating a safe space for people to post what brings them a little hit of joy each day, it would transform into a community of people helping each other find something to brighten their days. It started with being honest about a joyburst habit I was trying to create, and once I shared the story of one little baby owl, it grew into a Joyburst Movement. I was fortunate to have friends who jumped in and joined me in my joy parade and invited their circles to connect. You have to ask for help and have the courage to share your ideas, no matter how silly and small.

14. Giggle with a friend who appreciates the dorky side of you!

I make a big deal out of my birthday not to get well wishes, but because I love to spend time celebrating with family and friends.

On your own birthday, give yourself care, give your friends time, give a gift to someone or something that needs you.

Giver's Glow will look good on you.

Gramma Phyllis's
Chocolate Cream Pie

INGREDIENTS:

1 9-inch pie crust (baked and cooled)

1 package chocolate pudding (NOT instant)

1 C heavy cream

METHOD:

Cook pudding according to directions and pour into pie crust.

Cool in the refrigerator until the pudding is firm.

Top with real whipped cream and serve.

Sprinkle chocolate shavings on top of the cream.

Act Two:
Goodbyes and Grief

Someone once explained that grief comes in waves.
You first feel the shipwreck,
and you cling to the wreckage around you,
barely floating.

You hang on to a memory or a photo as you
bob along among your sea of tears.
The waves come without warning,
but then over time, they slow down
and feel further apart.

A song, a memory, or a picture can all
bring on a crash, and you are wrecked,
but you learn to get yourself back up.

Then you learn to predict the waves.
A birthday, a holiday, a movie, or the smell
of cake baking can knock you off balance.

You find that you get knocked down,
but then a beautiful thing happens.

You learn how to surf.

Rescuing Owlivia

Our neighbor Dale drives the windy roads home from the hospice care to his dark house. He turns off the lights like his wife Eleanor would remind him to do. He speaks out loud but to himself. He removes her favorite sweater and folds it on the chair, next to her sleeping cats.

"C'mon girls, let's get dinner," Dale beckons and both cats follow him into the kitchen.

The hoots sound closer and he wonders how close the owls are to his house. The cats crawl onto Eleanor's side of the bed, and he slips off to sleep.

The following day, he begins his chores of picking up fallen debris in his front yard. Among the leaves, he discovered a sweet little baby owl looking up at him. Owlivia, as he named her, chirped up at him, pleading for help. He called Todd and I over and we did what we could. I captured photos and shared videos with friends and family. Dale called local nature organizations for advice. Todd built her a nest in an antique drawer.

Todd spent the first-night transferring Owlivia to her new spot without imprinting his human scent. He attached a camera to the tree, and we waited. We worried that the mom would reject her or not be able to find her. I shared the footage and asked friends to send her positive thoughts and prayers.

I had salvaged the drawer being used for Owlivia's nest from a broken antique chest in my mom's home and planned to use it to serve sweets at our firepit. Todd saw a different use for the drawer and it began serving a new flock. The drawer was a piece of our family's Nantucket home that I rescued before selling the contents to another family. The chest of drawers was the first piece of furniture that my parents placed in their home, a gift from my grandparents.

We watched the mama owl selflessly feed the baby owlet, multiple creatures until she flew into her own nest. Dale shared that a second owlet had fallen the previous day, and he had buried him. My heart ached for this mama. Was there a hole in the nest that the babies fell from? Did Owlivia get pushed out by accident? Did she bravely think she could fly?

Todd called in an owl expert to examine Owlivia for injuries, and she explained that she was young enough to have her "egg tooth" on her beak. She encouraged Todd to stay out of the nest. Too much hovering with the owlet will cause stress and anxiety for the parents.

We all watched Owlivia preening her feathers and bonding with her parents. Owlivia's age of three weeks was determined after viewing her "egg tooth," which is used to break the shell of the egg and help the owl to escape from it at hatching. We learned something new each day.

As Todd shifted the camera angles, we watched them feed and connect. We replayed videos of her spreading her wings and testing her legs. She inspired us to start our days with a good stretch. I found myself pausing at the driveway to listen to the melody of hoots and screeches. The noises of these Great Horn Owls provided a whole new meditative experience.

The owls appeared to be in sync and connected to their young, but we had no idea what was going on in the big nest high in the sky. We tried not to make assumptions on what was happening behind the branches. As day turned to dusk, their harmony was comforting and we tucked ourselves in.

"Do you think the parents are happily enjoying time alone in their tree?" Todd asked.

"Are there other babies they need to take care of? Is Owlivia an only-owlet?" I wonder. Our pillow-talk shifted from our own nest to theirs.

Owlivia happily watched our neighbors walk, run, and bike by her tree. She appeared to enjoy her simple home and didn't shy away from the camera. Animals were an easy topic to share and talk about instead of the tired COVID conversations. Owlivia was featured in classrooms, at nurse's stations, Zoom meetings, nature volunteer groups, dinner tables, and bedsides. Times were tough for so many and people were subscribing to catch a glimpse of the sweet story of this bird.

She either fell from a nest that was not built properly, or she tried to fly too early. Either way, she landed in our hearts by mistake and that failure turned into our great joy. We tried to soak up her owl wisdom, looking forward to adding to this list before she flew away.

The Really Big Bird

When I make pancakes, I always burn the first batch. The pretty safe assumption is that it is a failure to wait for the griddle to heat up, but it might be due to the lack of prep. I have accepted my pancake cooking destiny and simply toss the first one into the trash and focus on the golden perfection of pancakes number three and four. Blueberries burst at the seams, butter oozing down the stack, and a signature "dipping pool" of syrup accessorizing my Instagram-worthy pancakes. Posting a photo helps me to savor my creation and inspires others to build their own pancake pile or head to their nearest diner for breakfast.

My first thoughts after waking up are often of my day ahead and the tasks that will follow. It takes an effort not to get dragged down by the burnt side of my day. Owlivia, our rescue owlet who lingered in our neighborhood one spring, helped me to flip my pancake.

The connections that were created thanks to our rescue owl are memorable. During the two months when I was greeted in the kitchen with video footage of Owlivia, my day would start with joy. Todd and I drank our coffee hunched over his phone as proud parents watched her midnight feedings. I would post the videos to social media and watch the ripple of friends, relatives, co-workers, nurses, teachers, doctors, and children enjoying watching her grow and thrive. We made new friends, connected with old ones, and watched relationships grow alongside her nest.

"We are listening to their hoots as we fall asleep each night. "

"Looking for an Owlivia update," the email begins.

"I played the video for my kindergarten class and they were mesmerized," a friend shared on the phone.

If I am going, to be honest, birds scare me. When a little chick-a-dee flies into our house, I become a shrieky damsel in distress. But this little creature was nothing to fear. When my motherly instincts kicked in and I worried about her, I relied on my social feed to share positive thoughts, prayers, and insights into owl behavior. It was during a time many of us were concerned for our own nests. Would our own children survive this time, would they fail, would they learn to fly after a year of lockdown? Owlivia gave us hope and a beautiful distraction from the crazy world around her tree. She gave us a happy connection that expanded across generations.

Thanks to a message from our friend Laura to a local newscaster Lisa Hughes, Boston's WBZ-TV came out with a film crew to hear our story. Reporter Lisa Hughes asked to meet Todd, Dale, and Owlivia; the rescuing trio. Dale was grieving his wife Eleanor who had recently passed away from a stroke and he was camera shy. We shared video footage of his discovery of the baby owlet in his yard and Lisa created a beautiful tale of the community coming together for this baby bird. I spent days reading the comments and continued to reshare, watching the joy ripples across communities.

I heard a noise at our basement door and I grabbed a bat, a young father in our neighbor shared. But when we crept down to check it out, we were greeted by a plump little Owlivia sitting at the door. We could hear her parents barking in the trees above warning predators of her vulnerable state.

The following week, another neighbor was preparing breakfast for her children when she heard a bump against their window. They pressed their faces to the window and watched Owlivia practicing her flight.

As she moved around our neighborhood, I walked with Dale and we chucked over how many families she was touching. I thought a lot about how joy can be spread and shared, but we have to find the moments and shine a light on them. There were so many layers from this one story, but we all learned the same message. Once you find a joyburst, sharing it makes it explode for others.

I will never forget what Owlivia looked like the day we met her. That little fluff ball with giant eyes looked like they were sewn on. The first time she smacked her beak into our camera was when she gobbled down a mouse in one bite, the way she watched her mama fly from the nest. Having to let Owlivia go was difficult, but I am grateful we had the time to appreciate her. She taught us to really observe nature around us, and reminded us that the gift is fleeting.

The memories we have made this part a little easier to swallow. I wrote her eulogy with Dale's input and framed my favorite photograph of Owlivia. We learned so much from her time with us, most importantly on how to flip our mindset each morning.

Owlivia's Final Flight

Her brother was crying in his highchair as little Eleanor was eating her oatmeal. She did not like the fat little raisins but she was too distracted by her brother to remove them from the bowl. They both jumped when the bird crashed into the window.

"Mama, it's Owlivia!" Eleanor squealed. Her brother clapped his sticky hands while Mama began recording the owl's test flights. Multiple times Owlivia would attempt a take-off, and then land with a thud. Eleanor bounced out of the kitchen, her red curls springing with every step as she made her way into the garage with her magic markers.

Good morning Owlivia, Brooks waved out the window as his mom lifted him from his crib.

"Did you make her b'fast?" he asked.

"No sweetie, her mom will take care of her," she explained.

When the sun set later that day, the mom looked out at Owlivia in the same flower bed and prayed that this was true. We all could sense that if she was not flying out of our neighborhood, something must be wrong. My heart broke for her mama who howled into the night.

"She can't be on her own," the vet explained. "It will be far too dangerous for her."

"Can't she just be with us and let us take care of her?" we ask.

"When you approach the cage, she is too anxious since she is blind. This is not about you, it is not fair to her." The medical team explained to us that Owlivia would need to be put down. We went through scenarios of keeping her as a pet and donating her to a Zoo, but they all involved life behind bars. Letting her go into the wild would be a cruel option since she could not defend herself. A blind owl who cannot see her predators would not survive in the wild. Based on her poor quality of life, the vet recommended putting Owlivia down and swiftly took action.

We played her videos and shared the beautiful photos taken over her six-week visit. We listened to more stories of people she touched. We focused on her, not on those she left behind.

For the first time I noticed that we have a lot of owl décor in our home, and so does my mom. At Christmas, I was given sweet gifts in her memory. The news station awarded the piece the "story of the year" and it was replayed on tv multiple times. I missed the excitement that her videos brought Todd and me each morning. I missed the joy of Todd sending the evening video footage to his parents, and our neighbor Dale, and then posting to social media feeds. Those ripples of joy created so many new connections and expanded our community at a time when we all needed to feel connected.

We watched for the next owl family. The dresser drawer, aka nest, remained in place. We were prepared to welcome another baby owl, should she land in our hearts again. Her nest may be empty, but her memories kept it warm.

TO OPENING
YOUR WINGS
AND CATCHING
WHATEVER
FALLS INTO
YOUR NEST.

RAISE YOUR GLASS

Life Lessons from Owlivia:

1. Be open and flexible to a new plan.

2. Believe in the power of prayer.

3. Embrace your failures.

4. Know when to back off and observe from a distance.

5. Shift your view and perspective.

6. Teach your chicks to care for themselves.

7. Listen carefully to the sounds of nature.

8. Do not make assumptions about what goes on in other nests.

9. Live simply, but find a good view.

10. Start your day with a good stretch.

***If you don't stop to
notice your surroundings,
you might miss the magic.***

If Once You Have Slept on an Island

If once you have slept on an island
You'll never be quite the same;
You may look as you looked the day before
And go by the same old name,

You may bustle about in street and shop;
You may sit at home and sew,
But you'll see blue water and wheeling gulls
Wherever your feet may go.

You may chat with the neighbors of this and that
And close to your fire keep,
But you'll hear ship whistle and lighthouse bell
And tides beat through your sleep.

Oh, you won't know why, and you can't say how
Such change upon you came,
But - once you have slept on an island
You'll never be quite the same!

~Rachel Field

The Gray Lady

I am grateful to my dear friend Jesse's grandmother Eleanor who invited Pookie to Nantucket Island as a young girl, introducing her to the magic of "the Gray Lady." Eleanor was a teacher at my mother's school and her daughter was a classmate. After two summer vacations with this family, my mother fell in love with the island. She lived on a farm with three brothers and her expectations were low. The third summer, Eleanor's older daughter Susan hired my mother to live in her home and cook and clean for a bunch of Harvard graduate students. My mother pretended to be able to cook and worked nights as a dishwasher, hitchhiking across the island since she was too young to drive. By the time my mom graduated nursing school, staying at Susan and her husband Walter's Nantucket home became a summer tradition.

Susan and Walter adopted their newborn son Jesse, the year before I arrived on the scene. Jesse and I shared funny adventures on our annual visits from learning to sail to writing a song about my lost tooth for the tooth fairy. Any memories I have of life before age ten involved Jesse and the Birge family.

My parents bought their own plot of island land on Dionis Beach, only to sell it a few years later when they wanted to renovate their kitchen in Belmont. Tom Nevers was an underdeveloped area of Nantucket and therefore there were less expensive homes for sale. My parents used my father's shiny new corporate American Express card and purchased a home on Wanoma Way and named her "Windswept." Both sets of grandparents tried to talk them out of this crazy purchase. In a stroke of fate, the builder asked to rent the house back from my parents for the first eighteen months. This move would cover the mortgage and enable them to buy the adjacent plot of land. Twelve years later, they were able to expand the home to fit our growing family. Eight years later, my parents renovated their bedroom for their retirement and created a playspace for their unborn grandchildren. My father oversaw this renovation project from his hospital yet he did not live to see the final product.

Everyone told them not to buy the house on Nantucket Island. They did not have the money but did have a vision of hosting their children at their own beach house. They rented the home to other families for twenty years, saving a few weeks each year for our family to enjoy it. When my father passed away at fifty-six, he altered their retirement road map. Despite being a scared young widow, my mom stayed the course and enjoyed many beach days, starry nights, and Thanksgiving dinners in that house. My parents' risk became our reward and I wear a necklace today reminding me of their journey.

I will never forget the way Windswept sparkled in the bright sunlight, twinkled at the stars at night, rested in the fog, and brought such joy. Windswept was the family project. We would travel together and go to the island to prepare the house for the next rental season. Not as happy as the Von Trapps, we would work together to scrub outdoor furniture, repair broken screens, weed the garden, refresh bedding, and replace lightbulbs. My parents would reward us with a trip to town for curly fries and burgers in the basement of the Brotherhood of Thieves.

As the years passed and our lives got busier, we would meet at Windswept each summer for a visit. My parents planned to retire and host their grandchildren in this home, but cancer rewrote their story. A decade after they bought Windswept, they were diagnosed with cancer within three years of each other and my mom survived, but my father did not. Keeping the house was a burden for my mom and each year she mentioned selling it. We helped her to keep it afloat.

One of our family traditions was to pack a turkey and a pumpkin pie into a cooler and ride the ferry over to Nantucket for an extended Thanksgiving Dinner. We would all arrive from our different pockets of New England the day before Thanksgiving. We would gather around the fireplace catching up, teasing each other as we often do. Four siblings, five years apart meant we were at various life stages, but on Nantucket, we would come together on common ground. We spent most of our time gathered in the kitchen where Pookie oversaw the boys baking Great-Gramma Phyllis's apple pie recipe. She would instruct Tyler to chop apples while instructing Mason on whipping dirty mashed potatoes. We hiked through the cranberry bogs while the meal was cooking. Football games and fireside naps followed the dinner. We stayed on the magical island for a few relaxing days, stretching the holiday into a family weekend getaway. It was my father's favorite holiday, and we were grateful to be able to share the home for eighteen years after his last Thanksgiving visit.

One of my father's dreams was to join the prestigious Sankaty Country Club, but he was placed on a long waiting list. The day after he died, a letter of acceptance arrived in their mailbox. It sat framed on his golf bag in lieu of a casket at his wake and funeral service.

Sixteen years later when we were on Nantucket for Thanksgiving, Tyler asked Pookie if he could work on the island and live with her the following summer. It took a lot of convincing since she did not want to spend her summer on Nantucket living with a teenager. But he called Sankaty and without any experience, was offered a summer job. The manager was impressed with him bravely showing up at the club on Thanksgiving weekend, asking for a chance. Tyler spent two summers living with her and quickly learned that the way to melt her heart was by bringing home Sankaty's chocolate-covered strawberries and making the club's famous cookies.

For twenty years, Pookie adjusted to her new life plan. Her adult children were not wallflowers, as she loves to explain to people. While we were all grieving our father, growing our own families, and riding the waves of life. We could not fault our mother when she finally decided to sell Windswept. Apres-Covid the real estate

Todd and I ferried over to Nantucket to create a moving plan and realized scattering my Dad's ashes off the bluff of the house was not the smartest idea. We literally sold his gravesite.

Todd does not plan; he takes a running start and leaps. He texted a contractor we had used previously and shared our predicament. We had a house of furnishings and everything was closed due to the pandemic. He texted a local family who had just moved from Mexico City and they came over and asked what we would be willing to donate. With my mom on the phone, we tagged a few treasures and divided up keepsakes. The family called their friends who quickly arrived in trucks. We helped them load their trucks with our furniture and I began to cry. It was happening too fast. A small boy held my son's plastic bat and walked over to me with his mom and aunt. They spoke Spanish so I could not understand, but they hugged me. The minister of their church arrived and explained that they had been living in the church basement since arriving from Mexico City and did not have furnishings. They were overwhelmed with gratitude and my tears turned to ones of joy. We helped the families fill multiple truckloads to their church and had the house ready for the next owners by the end of the weekend.

Windswept gave us thirty-eight years of memories. Three marriages, five grandchildren, and one island wedding. We lost a Dad, three grandparents, an aunt, a loyal dog Tucket, and two cats. We gained countless laughs and visits with friends and extended family. We have given my parents so much credit for taking the risk of buying the little home on the bluff, but it was my mother who introduced my father to the island of Nantucket. It was her friendship that got them their first invite to the magical island.

The poem my mom hung in the kitchen was correct. We were never the same after sleeping on that island. The next time you are considering bringing a friend on vacation, consider the possibilities. You never know who you might be inspiring.

When One Door Closes

The year my mom sold Windswept, we began to display little mementos in our own home. "Virginity" as we named the ship figurehead that watched over the living room for thirty years. I framed the needlepoints my mother created, along with my crooked attempt at the Nantucket skyline. We focused our energy on the joy of new recipes and not having to juggle holiday travel. We welcomed Tyler home from college and Facetimed my brother and his new little bundle of joy. We hiked on new trails in our town and used a stargazing app Tyler learned about in Vermont. We cheered Mason on at his high school football game with our friends. It is not the way we have celebrated in the past, but trying new traditions felt pretty good. But I missed the little gray lady, sugar donuts, and packing our car for a day of surfing the wild waves at Nobadeer Beach.

I had imagined a new family watching a movie together on our couch, or napping with a book on their chest. Nantucket is not something we can only enjoy because my mother owned a home. We rented a house for a week to return for our family's summer vacation.

We celebrated our anniversary at American Seasons, we took the boys out to Madaket Millie's for tacos, ice cream at the Juice Bar, beers at Cisco Brewery, and soaked up glorious beach days; some with sharks. For the cost, we could have taken a bigger family adventure, but I wanted us to experience the island again. I have been visiting Nantucket Island since I was six-weeks old, as a guest of the Birge family. My parents purchased their own home when I was thirteen: the same year I met Todd. For twenty-five years we spent a lot of time on the magical island and many of our family's best memories occurred with "the little gray lady," as Nantucket is affectionately called. After two years of not visiting her, it felt good to come home.

It took me a few days before I got the courage to drive out past the Serengeti to Tom Never's to visit my parent's home. We parked on the street and planned to walk out the path to the beach staircase. We were hit with a padlocked gate forbidding us to take a step further. We strolled down Wanoma Way trying to appear casual as I snapped pictures of the front yard. A woman in a jeep slowed next to us and asked if she could help us. When I explained that my parents owned her home for thirty years, she invited us in for a tour. "As long as you are okay with change because everything looks different," she warned. "Change is good," I replied as we walked through the door for the first time as a guest.

"Do the birds nest in the eaves?" Tyler asked. We hadn't noticed, but with wonder, she followed Tyler's point to a small bunch of baby birds peeking out of a nest tucked in the ceiling corner. Our fish door knocker welcomed us inside, but once we entered, everything looked brand new. They had whitewashed the woodwork, the floors, and the walls, creating a blank canvas for their modern decor. We followed the new owner around as she shared their plans for the home, dreams for the island, and memories they hope to create. They had not added signs of favorite spots, photos of beach days, shells they collected or blankets they napped under. I could close my eyes and imagine a game of Nantucketopoly strewn on the table, next to half of a puzzle, coffee in a chipped nautical mug, and Norah Jones playing softly on the stereo. This version of Windswept was not ours, and that felt ok. More than ok, it felt cathartic. I am embarrassed to admit that I mourned this home, and had been sad to say goodbye to the time we cherished with her. The home that I missed is not the physical structure, but the memories and items we collected and shared as a family. I did not visit our home.

Life is a pure flame,
and we live by an
invisible sun within us.

-Mary Ellen Chase, Windswept

Let's Talk

After living in Belmont, Massachusetts for thirteen years, our family moved to Potomac, Maryland for my Dad's job. I tried two high schools, landing at The Bullis School. I was furious over switching to a "snotty private school filled with drug dealers and sluts." Those are the exact words I spat at my father. I stayed in my shell at school and was a snappy turtle at home.

Moving to the country gave me an opportunity for new chores, and my favorite was driving the ride-on-lawnmower around the lawn. My father grew up above a funeral home in the city of Boston and marveled at the fact that he owned a lawn. A manicured lawn was a symbol of achievement and he expected me to care for our lawn with Pebble Beach standards. After each cut, he would inspect my work and I had to follow him with a weed wacker to trim any blades that I missed. To make this chore extra interesting, I suffered from severe pollen and grass allergies. By the time I would finish the process of making our lawn look golf course ready, I was a sneezing swollen-eyed mess. I would whine to my Dad who first would suggest we discuss the matter the following day, cleverly allowing for my allergy symptoms to disappear. His solution was to type up a contract of his expectations.

Worried that I was getting depressed, my mother insisted I see my school guidance counselor, Mr. Scott Votey. Mr. Votey had sympathetic eyes and a mustache that camouflaged his facial expressions. It did wiggle when I told him about the two-page contract my Dad had me sign over my lawn duties. In one study hall, I was caught passing a note to my friend. I had written about how a classmate's hair resembled pubic hair. As a frizzy-haired adult, I am not proud of this action, but I don't believe that she ever saw my insulting prose. Mr. Votey called my mother into our session and explained the infraction.

I caught a twinkle in his eye when he and my mother were stifling their laughter each time one of them said "pubic hair." As soon as I saw Mr. Votey's sense of humor, I could relax.

Mr. Votey encouraged me to try out for the school play and join the track team. I made two different groups of friends, LOVED being on stage, and discovered the joy of running, a habit I maintain today. At high school graduation, I was presented with the Joy of Living Award as my parents proudly sat in the audience. I hope to find Scott Votey to thank him for introducing me to the benefits of therapy.

When my parents both had cancer, when my Dad died, when I had postpartum depression, and when we struggled in our marriage, I searched for outside help. Often I have had to meet with a few therapists before finding the right one which makes it more challenging. My sister and I realized a few sessions in that a joint therapy session would not work since we couldn't talk about our relationship openly. Todd and I went to a guy who reminded us of Captain Kangaroo, but that did give us something to laugh about after the meetings. I have turned to friends and sharing a therapist gives us another way to connect. The gift of talking to someone outside of your circle is beneficial and my advice to anyone with extra items on your mind, talk them out with someone else.

Dance Like Everyone's Watching

"Who will I dance with?"

"Mummy, this isn't an event you need a date for," my mother explained to my Gramma Phyllis.

"Hmmpf, I also cannot believe my invitation was addressed to GRAMMA Phyllis. Now the mailman knows I am a grandmother! You are really making it very difficult for me to date," my grandmother criticized in the weeks before my wedding.

Single for the first time in her life, I now understand that my grandmother was anxious to attend my wedding while my grandfather was bringing a new girlfriend. Uncertainty triggers my own anxiety, but I have learned sharing my struggles and befriending her, helps me to manage. In Gramma's honor, I introduce friends and family to Anita; my anxious side. Anita was a friend of my grandmothers so the nickname reminds me not to be snarky when I get anxious.

At some point during the wedding reception, I made a comment to a college friend about my grandmother needing a dance partner. Sweet John McLean led Gramma Phyllis onto the dance floor and she crooned, "I have shirts older than you." Throughout our wedding video, Gramma can be seen twirling across the dance floor smiling as John spun her around.

Every single day I try to find a little thing to do for my anxious self. Anita loves to ruminate but when she gets started, I get her moving. I play music, I take her outside, and I force her to look up at the sky and breathe. Often by taking someone's hand, we can lead them towards joy.

"I hope you never
fear those mountains
in the distance,
never settle for
the path of
least resistance.
And when you get
the choice to sit
it out or dance,
I hope you dance."

~LeeAnn Womack

I Hope You Dance

Why aren't you dressed for work?

"I took the day off to visit you," I sheepishly explained.

"You need to go to work. Calling in sick is not going to help me get better. Go to work," my Dad preached from his hospital bed.

I nodded silently; you couldn't argue with him. I didn't explain that we were all afraid each week would be his last. Our family did not admit our fears or voice our anxiety as that would have been seen as negative. Instead, I dressed in my Ann Taylor pants suit and visited my Dad in the hospital, pretending I was on my lunch break.

A few weeks later, I strapped my newborn baby Tyler into his *Baby Bjorn* and we pushed my Dad in his wheelchair around the rehab center. I rattled on about Tyler's sleep habits, being back at work, and the latest episode of *24*. He asked me to check on the construction in Nantucket, share a resume of a colleague's daughter, and return a book to a friend. We focused on the drawings of the play space that was being built in his house for Tyler and the other unborn Colbert grandchildren. He had the blueprints across his hospital bed for the renovated bedroom that he and my mother would enjoy in their retirement.

My brother John arrived with pizza, per Dad's request. My mother came into his hospital room with my red boom box from high school. She slid the tape into the player and began dancing around the room to Lee Ann Womack's "*I Hope You Dance.*" We were annoyed that she was playing music and ignoring our somber moods. While our Mom wiggled into her signature dance moves, we hid our tears.

My father died a few months later, at the young age of fifty-six. I like to believe that his last weeks were spent focusing on what he loved. Dreaming of Nantucket with his family, helping others network into new jobs, passing along a book, and watching his wife dance.

The song always brings me back to my dad's last days, but the lyrics deliver a positive message that we cherish today. The memories of my Mom dancing around his hospital room also makes me smile.

Jack Colbert

The one summer I went to overnight camp the only care packages I received were the period pads my mom mailed me and one letter from my Dad. His letter was typed and signed "sincerely, Jack Colbert, jr." As he liked to say, "that went over like a lead balloon."

When I adopted the chore of mowing our lawn, Dad presented me with a contract. "Please agree to the terms of managing the grass and sign on the dotted line," he explained right before my mother stormed into his office and tore it to pieces.

But my most embarrassing memory from my tween years was when I was unloading the dishwasher in my new pale pink Izod shirt, frustrated as the steam fogged up my glasses and made the shirt stick to me.

"Sami, while you only have raisins on a cutting board, I think it's time for your mother to take you bra shopping."

I turned into Frose.

"You only need stamps and a piece of string, but it's time," he laughed. I walked out of the kitchen and heard my parent's arguing for a few hours.

When I share stories of my father, they have the death polish on them and I focus on the best moments. I don't remember when it happened, but that guy was not the same person who gave a memorable toast at my wedding. People can change. My Dad learned how his words had power and as a father, had a huge impact on all of us.

Missing Jack

We really didn't want to go to the engagement party, not because we weren't happy for the young couple, but because we weren't ready to socialize. We had seen many of the guests a month earlier at our father's funeral. The weeks following had been a depressing blur, and my mother, sister, and I were anxious about the onslaught of "how are yous."

We scanned the sea of faces as we entered the country club ballroom. Many sympathetic glances were directed our way and whispered about the family who lost their father to cancer.

"Where is Jack? I NEED to get him a gin n' tonic! Did he beat me to the bar?" An old neighbor quipped in rapid fashion without paying attention to our tense shoulders and sideways glances at each other in shock.

"There is no easy way to say this," my Mom stepped forward to explain while we braced ourselves. "Jack is dead. He died last month and we are doing OK." My mom chatted away while we watched this woman turn ten shades of crimson while she apologized profusely. Eventually, she walked away, never fully recovering. The four of us started laughing and could not stop, the tears feeling good. We moved to the bar and relaxed a bit. Until the former husband of the neighbor came up to us and asked, "Where's Jack?"

Together we turned away and left the party.

Today when I experience the "It's not fair to lose your father at thirty-one, the frustration over my sons not knowing their grandfather, and the general I-miss-my Dad feelings," I know how to lift the fog. I focus on the gifts he left me and his legacy that I hope gets passed down to his grandchildren. Writing out such a list is therapeutic.

1. One of the greatest gifts my Dad taught me was to be positive and to focus on the simple pleasures in life. He would pause at breakfast, sink his teeth into a warm buttery piece of Portuguese Toast and describe each delicious bite as he said "does it get any better than this?"

2. Find your inner cowboy. We took a family trip to Jackson Hole, Wyoming when his cancer took a nosedive. On the flight, he read us an excerpt from Annie Proux's book "Wyoming Stories," and asked us to call him Pake Bitts. He needed to reinvent himself to face this new challenge.

3. My Dad was a walking Facebook Page before it's time, always connecting with people to help them find a job, hire a babysitter, or get help on a home project. Anyway he could, he would network to connect those around him.

4. Rest and recharge. The man crammed more into a weekend than most would accomplish in a week, yet he would sit down for twenty minutes in front of a golf match on TV for a power nap.

5. Celebrate every chance you get. Knowing his survival rate was not strong, he enjoyed life to the end. When I was pregnant with our first son, my parents threw us a co-ed baby shower which my Dad turned into a dance party. I will never forget him hopping across the dance floor until the wee hours of the night like he didn't have a care in the world. That was the last party he hosted and it was a good one.

6. Do not give up until you find something you are good at. I was an awkward teen who could not find a sport I could play. Dad convinced me to join the track team and we ran on the weekends together. Although we did not talk openly about many issues, running alongside him made me feel closer to him. We ran many road races together, and to this day, I feel my Dad with me when I cross any finish line.

Our Dad

God loaned us a friend, his name was "Jack"
Then one sad day, he called him back,
We're glad we knew him for a little while,
We'll always remember that great Irish smile...

He was patient, kind, and stubborn, too.
But we wouldn't change a thing – would you?

Always ready to help,
both day or night,
It didn't matter,
Jack would make it right.

Oh, we'd have lively discussions, that's true
And if we were lucky, we'd even win a few.

So, grant Dear Lord, a peaceful rest
For the Friend that you loaned us
Was ONE OF THE BEST...

Jack "Pake" Colbert

March 22, 2002

Joy & Sorrow

Todd and I had plans to ski in Maine and I suspected and hoped this was the time. I sipped a beer and avoided the hot tub. As we drove out of town I asked Todd to stop at the pharmacy. We pulled off the next exit to find a bathroom and there in the restroom of Subway, I took a pregnancy test confirming that we were going to have a baby! My next pregnancy was not as easy. I spent two years seeing specialists, trying infertility drugs and being pricked and prodded to find a solution to my inability to conceive another child.

In her early fifties with a ten-year old daughter with a disability, my mother was not able to help me during this time. At twenty-five and twenty, my sister and brother were in different life stages and paralyzed in their own grief. Most of my friends were getting married, trying to get pregnant or following new careers. We had not experienced loss or this type of grief before.

At one point my mom's friend suggested that I show my mom extra compassion. My mother's breast cancer had rained on my college graduation, her chemo hijacked my move to Washington, D.C., and now I could not go to my mom about my own infertility. My friends with new babies had their mothers cooking and taking care of them and their new grandbabies. I was supposed to parent my mother and ignore my own grief. The hurt and anger made it pretty difficult to be a welcoming environment for a baby.

Twenty years and two sons later, I have a different perspective. My mother, who we call Pookie, is not a planner. She had four children, each five years apart, with Natalie arriving ten years after my brother John. She did not plan to be diagnosed with stage-four breast cancer two weeks before her first daughter graduated college. She did not plan to recover from an intense six-month treatment of chemo, to then become a caregiver for my father who was diagnosed with prostate cancer at forty-nine years old, Widowed at fifty-three, a recurrence of breast cancer, open-heart surgery to repair a heart-valve destroyed by chemo, she had to follow a new plan. Six grandchildren without my Dad by her side was not the life she dreamt of.

Pookie's strength is her ability to shift and adjust with an incredible sense of humor. We attended a dinner in my father's honor which was super depressing. Seeing members of his support group alive is a kick in the gut. But we laughed while we cried. Pookie can always find the humor in the absurd, and there is no one else I would rather laugh through my tears with.

Let Them Eat Cake

Grieving rituals give us a way to move forward with grief as a part of our lives. Many who lost loved ones during the Pandemic have not been able to hold public grieving rituals such as memorials or funerals, pausing the grieving process. Private rituals can be just as therapeutic.

We have held a golf tournament in honor of our father's love of the game, and to fundraise for the nonprofit he started. When I couldn't gather with friends inside for my milestone birthday in 2021, we celebrated on the course. I am not a big golfer myself, but it was a way to get friends together and feel connected to my Dad on my big day.

We struggled in the beginning on when to "celebrate" our father. On the first anniversary of his death, I framed a poem for my sister which she hung in her apartment. The following year, she met her now-husband Jonathan. On his first visit to her apartment, he paused at the poem, "Why is my birthday noted in this poem? What is the significance?" he asked.

"YOUR BIRTHDAY?" Sarah choked over the lump in her throat and was forced to explain that the day of his passing happens to be Jonathan's birthday. We joke that it's our father's way of making sure that my sister isn't too depressed on March 22nd.

Our father's birthday is a reason to celebrate and a better day to grieve our loss. We tested out activities in search of a new grief tradition. We went to my Mom's church and each made an ornament to hang on our trees. We watched his favorite movie, *Last of the Mohicans*, and cried through the soundtrack. One year I found a copy of his recipe for spaghetti sauce. Nothing fancy, but it was special to see his signature all-caps writing style. I got into a debate with my siblings over which meal was his favorite.

Since both Todd and my Dad's birthdays were the weeks prior to Christmas, we often held a joint celebratory dinner. That meant we needed a healthy dessert for my father and something chocolatey for Todd. As long as I knew him, my Dad made two desserts. Ice-box cake, which is layered whipped cream and chocolate sandwich cookies and formed into a log. His second dessert was whipped cream with Hershey's syrup, frosted over an angel food cake. In the holiday spirit, the chocolate angel food cake became Dad's signature cake. We needed it to be quick and not add to the stress of the holiday season. In a pinch, you can easily buy an angel food cake at the grocery store bakery, and frosting it with whipped cream makes it feel homemade. We glammed it up with chocolate shavings on top and angel food cake is known as healthy-ish. Once Sarah and Jonathan were engaged, we switched our focus to remembering our Dad on his birthday instead of his death anniversary. Each year since, Sarah and I have got together, baked his cake, and toasted our Dad.

Recently I called my childhood friend to check in on him since he lives alone in NYC. In his typical jolly way, Jason shared with me that he planned to celebrate his birthday, by attempting to recreate his late father's signature Black Forest cake. Jason lost his father a few years ago, and it warmed my heart to know that we share the same grief cake ritual. We laughed over my memories of seeing his father busy at the stove on Christmas Eve, and he reminisced over playing pool with my Dad on Christmas Day. He emailed me his favorite biscotti recipe and I attempted to bake them myself. How sweet that we are cities apart, friends since fourth grade, yet share a bond of grief baking. Connected while apart IS possible, we just have to get a little creative.

Use the Cancer

"You aren't wearing shoes?

"Nope, we aren't going far."

"What about your license? You should always drive with your license."

"Mum, I am fine. We are driving two miles for ice cream. Please stop."

I am short-tempered with my mother who is, in fact, right, but I am in too much of a rush to slow down and admit this fact. I buckle Tyler into the backseat and we drive down the sandy road to the 'Sconset Market.

We get our extra creamy cones of strawberry ice cream and get back into her Volvo station wagon. "Twenty is plenty in "Sconset," is the phrase locals slap on their bumper stickers. I am driving forty miles an hour through the quaint Nantucket village. As I am pulled over by the young Nantucket cop, I turn to my mom and quietly admit she was right. Now I am barefoot, without my license, driving DOUBLE the speed limit. As I roll down my window, Mom whips off her scarf and leans forward.

"Sorry, Officer, I had a break from chemo and my daughter wanted to treat me to ice cream."

"No problem Ma'am. Just try and take it slower next time."

I exhale.

"We might as well get something positive out of this. When in doubt, use the cancer," my Mom explains mid-lick of her cone.

When in doubt, use the cancer.

I Blame the Crab Cakes

The anniversary of my father's death is a week before my son Mason's birthday and a reminder of how the joy of motherhood was tangled with grief. My father died only five months after my first son Tyler was born. I learned how to pump, breastfeed and manage a newborn from the hospital as my Dad was dying of cancer. When I gave birth to my second son three years later, I rehashed my grief and suffered from postpartum depression.

Twenty years later, I am more equipped to deal with these feelings and approach the anniversary with a surfboard. I go for a run like I used to do with my Dad, and I look for red cardinals; a sign that he is nearby. I bake his signature angel food cake with chocolate whipped cream icing. I share photos with my siblings and laugh over the funniest stories we can remember. I've got this.

A few days later, we treat Mason to a fancy dinner to celebrate his birthday. The old style of the restaurant reminds me of my parent's country club. I order crab cakes. My Dad would have loved to be at that table with us and I am very sorry that my sons never met him. I share stories of how we never went out to restaurants with my parents. Only when they joined a country club was there a consideration that we might be included in a fancy evening out. The club membership was to enable him to network for his job and we understood that it was a privilege for him to practice his golf game. We waited until the last day of the month, and if my father had a minimum balance at their country club, we would get invited to dinner. He dangled that carrot inspiring us to want our own country club memberships. Once I was lucky enough to be invited to a table in the Grill Room of Brae Burn Country Club, I would celebrate with an order of their delicious crab cakes. I savored every last bite of that victory meal.

When the waiter delivers my crab cakes, tears roll down my face. Happy to be celebrating Mason's birthday, but missing one person at our table. That's the hard part about the waves of grief, they often come without warning. Some days you can be treading in the water riding the waves, but then other days you can step on a crab and be shocked by the pinch.

Doing the Best I Can

"Doing the best I can," is my mother's favorite phrase. The response can be useful in many situations, but I have found it to be a helpful holiday strategy.

When my Dad died, my Mom stopped hosting family gatherings, and my sister and I took over the responsibility. There were many dark holidays when we had to adjust to my father's absence, the years that my Mom was going through chemo, and the lowest point when she had open-heart surgery the week of Christmas. We were less than patient and would get frustrated if she couldn't attend a gathering. We gave her grief about her lack of effort when in reality, she was lowering our expectations of her. When you become a widow at fifty-three, battle two bouts of breast cancer, and then chemo destroys your heart, you learn not to bite off more than you can chew. She took our criticisms in stride, simply replying: "I am doing the best I can." We may not have understood it at the time, but not everyone has it in them to host holidays. My mom deserved to step aside and let us serve her.

Last week, we served Thanksgiving dinner to my in-laws. We have hosted in years past but as our guests have aged, we now find ourselves "serving" them. A hostess plans an event and entertains her guests while enjoying the party. Todd and I pinged bouncing against pongs, as we tried to find the mysteriously missing green bean casserole, manage the salad and apple crisps that were being created as guests arrived, pour wine, make Bloody Marys, and keep the oven and microwave working overtime. It was such a circus that we found ourselves laughing hysterically when Todd channeled Chevy Chase and overcooked the bird. We had to explain to one of our guests who was an exchange student from Venezuela that American family holidays are not all like the movie Christmas Vacation. I couldn't contain my giggles as I was eating dry Thanksgiving turkey for one minute and then found myself singing happy birthday to Todd's Great Aunt as we gathered around the rainbow cake my mother-in-law baked. No traditional pies for this holiday- we did the best we could with what our guests brought.

I went into our first holiday after a Pandemic-hiatus knowing it wouldn't be picture perfect. I thought I had delegated enough of the tasks to others, but after taking last year off, I had forgotten the amount of work it takes to host a holiday. When everything fell apart, I was happy to have a husband who laughed alongside me, and encouraged the rest of the family to join in. The dry turkey became the star of the show.

With busy to-do lists that are overwhelming, it is a difficult time to stay sane. I plan to keep my expectations low and remind everyone around me, I am doing the best that I can. Thanks, Mum.

Bye, Bye,
Mr. American Pie

Many of us who have been married for a long time become bitter over gift-giving at the holidays. I am not sure why, but when I got married, I took over the role of Santa, purchasing all of the gifts that our family gave to others. I am sure that it was exciting at first, but over a period of years, it has become a burden (sorry Greenfields). Last year, in a frustrated moment, I suggested that Todd help me with a gift for his own parents. My in-laws are the most gracious people I know, and they refuse most gifts, thinking they are unnecessary or extravagant. They just want the gift of our presence, which makes the selection of an actual present challenging.

Todd reviewed what we have given them in the past and came up with the idea to sign them up for a meal delivery service. His mom loves to cook, and his Dad loves to eat, so this sounded like a great plan. To be honest, I was just happy to not have to shop for another gift. We sent them the gift of *Blue Apron*, and Todd spent hours Facetiming his father to teach him the ins and outs of how to select meals. Todd also added boxes of wine to the order, which were selected to pair with the meals and scheduled for weekly deliveries.

Twice a week I would walk into Todd's home office where his Dad would be on his screen gushing over their latest dish. His mom sent photos of their table including a white tablecloth, lit candles, a bottle of wine and proudly presenting their latest culinary accomplishment on two plates. My father-in-law would greet the delivery person in the driveway and quickly unpack the crate like a young boy on Christmas morning.

"It looked so good, I had to start the salmon before Mary got home!" he texted. "Wow, I have never eaten bok choy, but it pairs so nicely with the Rose they sent."

In thirty years of us being together, I had only witnessed my father-in-law grilling and drinking bourbon, so this came as a pleasant surprise. For many months this gift gave Todd a daily connection with his parents and he saw a side of his Dad he had never seen before. On Valentine's Day they texted over the joy they shared cooking scallops and enjoying the new wine together for a dinner they created. Their stomachs, and our hearts, were full. We could not have imagined that just two weeks after Valentine's Day my father-in-law's heart would fail and take him from us.

We spent many days sharing stories and gathering photos of our time with him, and many of those involved his newfound cooking skills. At his funeral, Todd stood before the church filled with our family and friends who came to show their love. He delivered the most heartfelt eulogy filled with laughter and tears from the memories that were created by his father. Todd's mom sat proudly in the front pew of the church, holding my hand and gushing with pride as Todd exited the altar. "Thanks for giving Dad that gift" she whispered when a teary Todd returned to our pew.

I think Todd nailed the gift-giving this year.

Here's to drinking in all that today will bring.

CHEERS!

Bobby G.

Many of our friends refer to my husband Todd as MacGyver, but Bobby G. was the true O.G. There wasn't anything he couldn't fix, and he taught his sons how to problem solve through any repair. A dry cleaner by trade, his business skyrocketed with his attention to detail and love to put everyone's needs in front of his own.

When Todd's sister had cancer, Bobby shared her experience with a diagnosis the same week. They could text each other daily and share in their recoveries and in typical Greenfield family style, by both kicking cancer's ass.

I lost my father when our first son was only five months old, and Bobby stepped in to be double grandfathers. "You are their ONLY grandfather," I would guilt Bobby into attending in honor of both fathers. He didn't miss a football or rugby game with the boys and played their piano videos on his iPad each day. My dad got me through the formative years and had the joy of seeing me graduate from college, fall in love with Todd, and then walk me down the aisle at our wedding. Bobby took the baton and I was lucky to have him for the twenty years of having his grandsons, our homes, careers, and many memories.

For each article I wrote, Bobby would call to comment on it, and share his thoughts which was an unexpected surprise. Bobby loved to tease me and kept me laughing on the darkest days. When we spent time with the rest of the family, he was giddy with excitement. He loved hearing the stories of the cousins playing together.

He emailed Todd to share his rapidly declining health. I can't remember ever getting an email from him before. It was in his own Bob-speak: crisp, brief, and to the point. He had so much love inside, that it was going to burst. I had so many quick sarcastic interactions with him, that this act did not surprise me. Todd could ask if he was ready, but his father did not want to discuss it anymore. This was the plan he had decided on, and we could follow it or step aside.

We were sad to lose him, but also knew that this was the way he wanted to go. He had driven to Todd's brother's to deliver warm cookies that Todd's mom had just baked. A few steps into their kitchen, he was quickly gone. When we met the ambulance at the hospital, I leaned in to kiss his head one last time. He electric shocked me, and I smiled with that final zinger from Bobby G.

We stood in his closet the following day trying to pick out what he would wear to his wake. Bob's jeans hung pressed next to his shirts in the very organized fashion of a retired dry-cleaner.

"My Gramma Phyllis was buried in her favorite bathing suit," I blurted out. Todd, his sister, and I broke into a fit of laughter. It was just what we needed.

Funeral Lessons

"You cannot read his eulogy; you'll be way too emotional.

"It will be so hard. You won't be able to focus; you'll be so nervous."

"You will miss out on the service as you stress about speaking."

"There is going to be a HUGE crowd."

Todd and his sister Jodi tried to sway me, but my mind was made up. Over many beers and tears, John and Sarah helped curate our memories and his famous quotes. My siblings helped me to paint a picture of our father, on his way to heaven. It was difficult and I was very emotional. I asked to speak first so I wouldn't be as nervous, and so I could listen to the speakers who followed me. I saw my siblings crying in their pews, but locked eyes with Todd and was able to deliver my speech. I returned to my seat and openly sobbed in my pew when a local sportscaster sang 'Swing Low Sweet Chariot," but also felt such a release. It brought me peace to share my piece.

Recently a friend asked me to read a eulogy she was struggling to write for her dear friend who just passed away. I went right back to that moment, gripping the podium, looking into the sea of an overly packed church.

"Speak from your heart. Share your favorite memories of her. Her daughter will want to hear of the fun you had together. Tell her story from your point of view and the church will listen. Sit outside with a notebook and just free flow and do not stop to critique yourself," I suggested.

She sent me her first draft and it was beautiful because it was her story. I gave her a lot of praise and encouragement so she would not stress, or change her mind. You need as much confidence as you can to get up and share your heart with others. I know this from experience. I reminded her to feel her friend's presence, and have faith that she was listening. She proudly texted me after her send-off, and I could feel her joy. When I saw her, I asked about her friend and we shared a new connection.

When my friend Bryson's father passed away, I watched his funeral via FaceTime from my living room. My son walked into the room as

I was listening to the stories, and I shared my memories with him. "Row your own boat," was one of my favorite phrases that Bryson's dad taught me to use when our boys were small and would tattle on each other. Years earlier Bryson had shared a sermon he wrote with the Dr. Seuss theme of "Oh the places you go." I read that to my family and we shared our own toast to her father, an opportunity I wouldn't have had if I wasn't watching his service via my computer.

It's true, I love the shivah portion of death. We aren't Jewish, but the space in time when you are planning the funeral arrangements, gathering photos, and telling stories is very therapeutic. My niece pulled up videos on her phone of my father-in-law and we all laughed. We found a series of selfies he took of him and the various granddogs, seeing a side of him many of us had missed.

You will be incredible, just speak from your heart. You have written beautiful words. Heart-dump your thoughts about him on paper and then go back and stitch them together. Todd asked my brother-in-law and me to read his eulogy draft and we continued to boost his courage with support. While Todd wrote his parent's dining room table I showered him with sweets, beers, and kisses as I passed by. When he got frustrated over distractions, we moved to our own house, despite his family wanting him front and center. We crawled into bed, and the next morning set him up with a new writing spot; our kitchen counter.

When he took breaks to fix our dishwasher, or to run to Home Depot to buy a spring to fix our water dispenser, I didn't convince him that these repairs were not necessary, I started his car. When he was rehearsing in front of the bathroom mirror, in his car, and in his office, I poured him a glass of wine and baked us focaccia bread, my own ways to cope with anxiety. I never told him it was good enough or convinced him to stop, I gave him his space. Every time he doubted his ability to deliver the eulogy, I cheered him on.

"I can't look at the grandchildren's row or I will lose it," Todd whispered to me in the front pew of his father's funeral. "I want to look at Jonathan but your sister crying will be contagious. Find me someone to focus on." I craned my neck and scanned the crowd behind us. I saw another Bob in the family.

"Focus on Bob; he is smiling and has a cute shiny bald head. Bob will be your beacon of light" I whispered.

Todd stood before the church filled with his own family and friends who came to show their love for his father. He gave the most touching eulogy I have ever heard and I sat proudly in the front row, holding hands with his mother.

"Thank you for giving Dad and me this incredible gift," she said to Todd as he slid back in the aisle. Bob was his beacon.

I love the advice that my friend Tara gave me to pass along to Todd after his Dad died. "Enjoy today, it is one chance you have to see everyone who loved your Dad in the same space. Ask for stories, listen deeply, savor the experiences he shared with others." Todd took that advice to heart and spent the luncheon following the funeral shaking hands and collecting stories from an era before his father was a Dad.

At a local member of our community; Ando's funeral last year, multiple speakers shared his hidden laundry talents. Ando was our son's high school trainer and laundry was not a skill we would expect to hear about at his service. My towels have never been fluffier thanks to his recommendation to wash them in a separate load.

On Tyler's freshman move-in day at U.V.M., we stood in a long line, nervous about leaving our firstborn to connect with fellow students in a socially distanced sea of masks. We recognized an Ando's Army t-shirt on another boy and made the connection with him.

That's the nice thing about funerals, eulogies not only tell the stories of those we have lost, but they also teach us where to look for their angels in the future.

> Enjoy the funeral;
> it is the one chance you have
> to ask for stories, listen deeply,
> and savor the experiences
> of your loved one.

Nudges and God Winks

I began unloading the car, swallowing the lump in my throat. I love spending time with our son Tyler, and it was going to be a few months until we saw him again. This is the hard part. I am so excited for him to begin college again, but letting go isn't easy. Tyler chuckles as he balances a stack of milk crates overflowing with hangers, a hammock, protein powder, and Christmas lights. All the necessities for his dorm. "Ahhhh Ando," Tyler sighs and points to a small sticker on the back of a jeep. We stop to look closely at the logo and remember our town hero who lost his battle with cancer two Christmases ago. Last year at UVM move-in, we saw a t-shirt with the same "Ando's Army" logo. I stop to consider what his wife is thinking as she is navigating this process without her husband, and she will do it for each of their four children.

In our family, we refer to these moments or angel nudges as "God Winks." Forcing us to pause and be grateful for the moment we are experiencing. A little second where we are reminded of someone who is no longer with us, who might be sending us a message. I used to feel that every time I saw a red cardinal, it was my Dad visiting me. I saw them when I was outside running, an activity we enjoyed together. I didn't see the bird often, but each time I did see one, it felt like Christmas morning.

My sister Sarah had her wedding on Nantucket Island, our family's happy place. The sadness of my Dad's absence was difficult to navigate on such a joyous occasion. Todd and my brother walked her down the aisle, all three of them trying to smile through their tears. An orange butterfly landed on her wedding dress, and when she reached the altar, another two landed on her shoulder. The sun sparkled along the ocean's edge and a pair of seals treaded water appearing to be watching the ceremony.

Be sure to pay attention to God's winks.

Grief Stones

I haven't brought up her Dad because I don't want to remind her and bring her down." Many friends would say this to Todd after my Dad died at the young age of 56.

"He is always on her mind, and she is looking for an excuse to bring him into the conversation" would be his reply. That was the best gift Todd gave me. We were just shy of 30 and lost in a sea of grief, but sharing stories of him helped make each day a teeny bit easier.

When I ask a friend who is recently widowed, she explains that the hardest moment is when people around her avoid the elephant in the room. She desperately wants to talk about the big missing elephant. Of course, everybody grieves differently, but for me, sharing stories made me feel like my Dad was still close.

Another friend often reminds me that when facing an overwhelming problem, "an elephant cannot be swallowed in one bite." This metaphor helps me to break up a problem into digestible bites. Maybe grieving a loved one is the same? Keep them close by sharing small stories, and slowly adjust to life without them present.

Like many people, I see a cardinal and think of my Dad. At my sister's wedding, an orange butterfly landed on her wedding dress and it took our breath away. I have only seen a monarch butterfly like that on that day.

When I snuggle on our couch, wrapped in the blanket that Gramma Phyllis knit for our wedding present. I text my sister and brother and they too are snuggling in their blankets from her. We joke that she didn't hug but instead made us hugs knit from yarn.

When I wear my necklace made from my Dad's cufflink, when I walk by the figurehead from my parent's Nantucket home, when I see my framed photo of Owlivia, they all comfort me.

I have a friend who believes her Dad drops pennies from heaven and another who sees feathers as her sign. Some mention feeling their angels when they dream, waking up feeling like they saw their loved one. I am fascinated by other people's grief stones and enjoy the stories of feathers, birds, pennies, and butterflies. The object or animal is not important, it is the feeling that they deliver. Like a love note delivered straight to you letting you know that you are seen and everything is going to be alright.

When Owlivia flew her nest there were a few days of despair and we all felt her absence. Then a young kindergartener in our neighborhood ran off her school bus when she spotted Owlivia sitting on a nearby rock. Her name was Eleanor and she could not believe her good fortune!

Owlivia was a special omen, reminding Todd and me that as a team, we can make other people feel good. My mom calls us magnets, drawing people in with our positive force. That is one incredible pull.

*Sorrow prepares you for Joy.
It violently sweeps
everything out of your
house, so that new joy can
find space to enter. It shakes
the yellow leaves from the
bough of your heart, so that
fresh, green leaves can grow
in their place. It pulls up
the rotten roots, so that new
roots hidden beneath have
room to grow."*

~Rumi

My Two Dads

Tyler Jack was born at 8:01 p.m. and all four grandparents were in the waiting room together. Twenty years later, I realize how lucky I am to have had that unique experience. The night was a blur and I eventually settled into my hospital room after twenty-four hours of labor.

I rode through the roller coaster of hormones the next day. Numerous nurses taught me to breastfeed while Todd focused on mastering the swaddle for our new little bundle of joy. We walked the hospital hallway and took a bathing class together. Midway through the class, I couldn't stop crying. It felt overwhelming. I left Todd and shuffled back to my room. My Dad was sitting in his signature Brooks Brothers suit and tie, chatting with my father-in-law, clad in his jeans and comfortable sweater. I hid my tears, embarrassed that I was feeling anything but sheer happiness.

"C'mon honey, time to feed your son again," the nurse rolled the bassinet into the room so I could breastfeed Tyler. I tensed up, my mind swirling as I tried to remember the instructions the other nurses gave me.

"You guys need to leave," I squeaked over the lump in my throat. I could not breastfeed like they do in the movies, subtly without any boob peeking out.

"No problem, I brought Bobby and my lunch," my Dad replied. They spun their chairs around so their backs were facing my bed. They began unpacking their subs and catching up on news like I wasn't in the room. The nurse helped me to adjust Tyler and relax my death grip. My Dad told my father-in-law jokes and they laughed as they ate their lunch together. Tyler latched on and the nurse slipped quietly out of the room. I fed my son while listening to their chatter. Todd bounced in and shared what he learned in bathing class. The fathers teased Todd for being such an enthusiastic new Dad. I relaxed my shoulders as we fell into a groove; their chatter music to Tyler Jack's newborn ears.

Send it

Nothing brings out people's true colors like a tragedy. I am not suggesting that a tragic experience is enjoyable, but when heartbreak hits, you truly see the good rise to the top. Certain friends will go out of their way to make you feel better, and it is their support that helps get you through the bad days.

I am a list girl and kept track of what has been the most helpful to our family after loss. Obviously, each person is different, so feel free to add your own flavor to this list of ingredients.

1. As soon as you hear, reach out. Do not pass go, do not collect $200, just connect. It does not hurt to say, "I do not know what to say." That counts and might be just what your friend wants to hear. Send the text.

2. Show up. We had friends who bought groceries, and sent or made food without asking if we needed it. Flowers and booze also bring out joy. Just send it.

3. Help with kids by offering rides, play dates, and over-nights. It not only helps the parents but gives the kids time with their friends which they probably need.

4. I called my mom in tears the day after we lost my father-in-law, and she drove right over. My Mom had not done my laundry since high school, but she dove into the overflowing baskets. This did include a lesson on our machine first, and then she fell into a groove of washing anything she could find in our house. There was something so soothing about my Mom folding laundry next to me on the couch which lulled me to sleep. If General Hospital was on, I would have felt like we were right back into the late 80s.

5. Take care of domestic chores. I was fortunate enough to take a day off of work before the funeral and a friend gave me this

advice. I carried a note in my pocket to keep me on track. Prescriptions at CVS, cancel SAT, reschedule flights, go to the bank, and post office. It felt good to check off tasks before the next few whirlwind days of funeral planning.

6. Move. I never regret squeezing in exercise. Neither does my anxiety.

7. Gather photos. This is one of my favorite things to do since the stories leap off the pictures. Do this with friends or family to share your memories of the deceased.

8. Enjoy the funeral. You are given one day to see all the people who loved your Dad. Listen to the stories, ask questions about him, soak it up, and savor this gift. My friend Tara shared this advice she got at her Mom's funeral and it was the greatest gift. I watched Todd talk to everyone after his Dad's funeral and learn a lot about the relationships that his Dad had without him.

9. Spend time with those left behind. They want to talk about the person they lost and bringing it up will not remind them of their loss. It is always on their mind so ask questions and let them share their stories.

10. Savor your own experiences as someday they could help someone else. Empathy is a powerful fuel that will push you through together. We stood in my father-in-law's closet, discussing what had been selected for him to wear to his own funeral. His jeans hung pressed tightly next to his pants in the organized fashion of a former dry-cleaner. Nothing is sadder than looking at the belongings of someone who has recently passed away. "Gramma Phyllis was buried in her gold bathing suit," I blurted out. It was absurd, but she spent her free time slathering her leather skin in Bain de Soleil and floating in her pool. Her bathing suit was her favorite outfit. We laughed hard.

11. Read the above list, rinse and repeat. Three months after any tragedy, people forget and move on with their own lives. Your friends need you to never forget.

The Boy Next Door

My husband, Todd spends most of his free time working in our yard. As soon as he heads outside, he is joined by his two buddies. One has floppy ears and wags his tail, and the other is the neighbor Todd calls "Fifty-one." It is heartwarming to see them sitting on logs taking a break to burn the tree limbs they've collected.

On many Saturdays, Todd and Fifty-One, or Dale as he's commonly known, are side-by-side stacking wood with Simba wagging his tail between them. They compare early morning gym routines, they share college stories, and they laugh over the many pranks they've pulled. Fifty-One stacks wood for our fireplace and is outside early t on the day Todd rents a log splitter, excited to join in the fun.

When Simba goes missing, as he sometimes does, we look in Dale's garage first and typically he is at the workbench enjoying a snack, or on the deck catching the popcorn Dale's wife Eleanor has popped for the birds. Simba loves that Dale keeps treats in his coat pocket and scratches his back with his rough work gloves. The same gloves that Todd replaced earlier this year, framing the old ones for his garage as a trophy of their yard work.

"This is all your land," Dale explains to Todd as they stack a woodpile that will last until we have grandchildren. "Fifty-one percent of it is yours, I own forty-nine" Todd responds. Their nicknames are born.

If we are working late, Dale happily takes care of Simba, texting us the details of where they walked and what they dropped behind. He watches our house when we go out of town, and isn't ruffled by a group of boys in the woods we share. This is not his first rodeo: he has three grown sons of his own.

Three weeks ago, his bride of forty-eight years was rushed to the hospital and did not return. Watching Dale experience his loss like so many who have lost loved ones during COVID, was heartbreaking. Our neighborhood came together to help him with meals, took him for walks, and taught him a few helpful domestic chores.

"Those cookies were heavenly," Dale thanked me on a recent visit to our porch. "Todd and Mason get the credit," I explained. "You bake?" he asks Todd. "Your gen-eration amazes me," he laughs. Dale explains what he has learned in his three weeks as a bachelor and it makes me appreciate having a husband who is not afraid of the kitchen.

I look out our window and see Dale feeding some birds popcorn, adopting Eleanor's chores. Simba and I take him on a walk, stopping as he delivers treats to all of the dogs in our neighborhood.

Like my favorite elderly character Carl from the movie Up, Dale is now forced to create new routines. He is upbeat as he tells me about the dinner he made and plans he has to clean out the attic. He has adapted quickly to being in charge of turning out lights when he leaves a room, feeding their cats, and doing the laundry. He is proud of his scrambled eggs and he has invited the cats to sleep on Eleanor's side of the bed.

Like Russell in the movie, I would like to bestow Dale with the "Ellie badge" for his courage to take on this new adventure. I know that Eleanor is proudly watching his every move as he celebrates their forty-eighth wedding anniversary alone.

Fill the Gap

I finally understand why the retail chain chose the name "The Gap" for its clothing line. Have a chorus concert at school? Then run to The Gap for a pair of khakis. Dressing up for a piano recital? Purchase a tie, a dress shirt, or even a pair of socks in the store. All done in just one stop. The Gap has been the store that has fulfilled many last-minute purchases for us.

A week ago, my son Mason came home from football practice with a swollen thumb. After icing it throughout the evening, he asked for a hand brace. At 10 p.m., the resources for orthopedic products are limited. As I searched online, my "working mom guilt" kicked in as I knew I couldn't drive around the following day to find him a remedy, nor could Amazon fill in for me. The next day, on my way home from work, I tried two local spots but no one had hand braces in stock. I drove home deflated. To my surprise, Mason came home from practice proudly wearing a hand brace!

"Don't worry Mum, Coach Finn helped me out," he explained. "He not only taught me how to tape my thumb, but he bought me this brace and gave me a few exercise balls to strengthen the surrounding muscles."

Who is this angel? Coach Finn retired and recently joined our high-school football team as a volunteer coach. Did he somehow know the stress I was feeling over not being able to help my son? Was this injury a big deal? No, but his kind gesture filled a huge gap in our home and eliminated a lot of stress. Coach Finn filled a gap.

When my son was an infant, my mother-in-law would come to visit and help care for us. When I was feeding our baby, she would grab a large glass, fill it with ice water, add a straw and place it next to me. I never asked for a drink, but gulped down the refreshing glass which she would then magically refill. She filled a gap.

Tragedies are picking up speed and we all know too many people who are struggling with something. We don't need to fill the gap, we should take Ryan Gosling's advice from the movie "Crazy, Stupid, Love" and "be better than the Gap." When you head to the store, do you offer to grab a friend something they might need? When you see an angry mom, do you give her a big smile and not judge? When you are done with sports equipment, do you pass it along to a younger athlete? Filling the gap can be done in small gestures or through your body language, and this type of gap doesn't cost a thing.

Pake Bitts

Dear Dad,

This time reminds me so much of 9-11 and the first time I heard you cry when you called me as we watched the towers on TV. You were so distraught for the people fleeing from those buildings, and you worried about your own staff in Boston. I track how long you have been by all that has happened. You have gained five grandchildren, a son-in-law, and a daughter-in-law. You loved your palm-pilot and would be blown away with the iPhone, Apple Watch, and AirPods. You would get excited today over the way people are learning to connect virtually.

The week before the pandemic exploded, I was driving to work thinking of how excited you would be to have me working in your town. You would have spent your time being sure to connect me with anyone you came in contact with and your networking skills were legendary. And *Sweetgreen* would have made you so happy! How I wish I could meet you for a quick lunch. That day my coworker asked me to ride with her to pick up lunch for our office. When I got into her car, I felt your presence. On her passenger seat was *Close Range, Wyoming Stories* by Annie Proulx. Sarah explained that for some strange reason, she had not returned the book her husband had taken out of the library. I told her the story of your bucket list trip to Jackson Hole when you realized that your cancer had spread and the future looked bleak. On that flight, you asked us to start calling you *Pake Bitts*, a cowboy character from Annie's book. You believed that you needed to adopt a courageous cowboy character so you could kick cancer's ass. You were going to become Pake Bitt, and we laughed so hard as we teased you. As things always do in the Colbert family, it became a running joke on the trip, and we even made up nicknames for Mum to accompany this silly idea. When we returned from Jackson Hole, and I became pregnant with Tyler, we decided that "Pake" was a more suitable name than Grandpa. And "Pookie" would be his trusty sidekick. We have all told this story often since you passed, and we never called you Dad again. I've read the book and realized that the character was not a brave role model, but you must have liked his name and wanted some of his swagger.

When authors write their stories, I expect they plan to touch their readers, but do they ever really know the effect their book may have? Twenty years after first hearing of this book, we are still talking about it and re-reading it. The older I get, the more I enjoy reading and find books to be a wonderful escape. To all of the writers out there, please do not stop sharing your gifts. Especially with all that is going on in the world today, you never know who might need to hear your story.

Coming Out

The night my cousins and I learned that our aunt was a lesbian, we could not avoid gay slurs. Our aunt patiently corrected her gaggle of awkward tween nieces, while her girlfriend offered us talk therapy. We had spent time with our aunt's girlfriends, not truly understanding the depth of their relationships.

I am grateful that Aunt Pat was brave enough to come out to our family. It couldn't have been easy, and while I remember everyone being accepting, it's possible she perceived the reaction of her Irish catholic differently. For a year prior, she had pretended to be engaged and often talked about her wedding plans. My Dad invited an eligible bachelor to our family's Thanksgiving Dinner, clueless about both of their sexual preferences (Dad later learned the potential suitor was also gay).

I was living a very sheltered middle school life until Aunt Pat changed my perspective. She was a sarcastic, quick-witted, very successful businesswoman who owned her own home and boat. She shattered any stereotypes I may have had about lesbians, and because I loved Aunt Pat, that act of bravery encouraged me to open my mind and heart. Our gift from God was a former nun Ros, who changed my aunt's life. Ros was softer-spoken and mellowed-out Aunt Pat. She was the best listener and a breath of fresh air for our family. It also helped that she had a very strong golf game and could beat my father; Aunt Pat's brother.

When Ros's cancer took a dramatic turn for the worse, my cousins called to let me know. Aunt Pat suggested we visit while Ros was still alive, instead of waiting to attend a funeral without her physical presence. We had the best visit. My cousins, sister, and I flew down and immediately went to the grocery store to fill our cart with fruit, yogurt, chips and salsa, wine, and Titos. Our version of a hospice picnic basket.

We set up our snacks and bar poolside, and lounged underneath Ros's bedroom window. We each took turns visiting with Ros, and then regrouping in the pool for group tears and therapy. Everything we would have said about her at her funeral, we were able to say to Ros in her bedroom. We laughed a lot and cried more. Ros laid in her bed, listening to us through her window, and drifted in and out of sleep. Aunt Pat shared her fears of losing the love of her life, and we tried but couldn't dry her tears (we were in a pool).

Two weeks later, Ros passed away and Aunt Pat held a small service for their friends. It was the most selfless act to have us visit before since it left her with less support during the ceremony. It is a gift from Aunt Pat that I will never forget.

The Bucket List

Buy a Jeep, get a lab puppy, name the puppy after our happy place, and plan an epic family adventure. Diagnosed with cancer at 49, my dad's Bucket List kept our family engaged in positive experiences during those dark days.

I had not heard of a Bucket List before, but as my Dad announced that step one was for us to go to Jackson Hole on a summer vacation, I jumped on board. On the flight, my Dad asked us to start calling him "Pake Bitts," a cowboy character from Annie Proulx's book; "Close Range: Wyoming Stories". He explained that he wanted to adopt a courageous cowboy character to help him kick cancer's ass. We laughed and teased him over the idea of calling him anything but Dad. As things always progress in our family, it became a running joke on the trip, and we even made up nicknames for my Mum to accompany this silly idea. When we returned from Jackson Hole, and I became pregnant with Tyler, we decided that "Pake" was a better name than Grandpa. "Pookie" would be his trusty sidekick. We never called him Dad again.

When my mother was battling her second bout of breast cancer, I wrote and drew cartoons through my pain. I created a storybook I could read to my young sons to explain what we referred to as the "cancer monster," who was stealing their grandmother's energy. In the storybook, the boys created their own "Summer Bucket List" to follow on their vacation:

- Catch sand crabs at the beach.

- Eat ice cream cones on the dock.

- Plant a vegetable garden.

- Bake great-grandma's blueberry pie.

- Bike to town for sugar donuts.

I found it therapeutic to write about our experience and spent a decade editing and drawing our emotions as they hit. I am not a psychologist, but this exercise certainly helped us cope.

During the weird summer of COVID, we had masks on, masks off, our happy place was sold, and even the weather felt different. At the end of June, I tried writing my own Summer Bucket List:

- Try something new each week: a recipe, a workout, or say "yes" when offered an opportunity.

- Do not over plan- keep space for spontaneity.

- Nap every chance I get.

Reviewing the list at the end of the season helped me to re-frame it in bright light. I spontaneously packed my overnight bag and visited friends. I read and napped in the afternoons, a luxury I typically reserved for vacations. I tried boxing and fell in love with beet hummus.

I walked into work and asked a colleague how her weekend was. She immediately referenced a Summer Bucket List on her phone and proceeded to read aloud the items. She had completed three goals and left four untouched. Her perception of the last weekend of summer was positive and productive and she felt a sense of satisfaction over her accomplishments. I shared my own weekend highs: books, beet hummus, boxing, Bullfinches restaurant, and some bubbly booze.

Whether you create a Bucket List at the end of your life, or as a seasonal activity, it can be a source of joy. Different from your goals, it can be a way to document the dreams and adventures you hope to experience. While I love the smell of suntan lotion, I am looking forward to creating a Fall Bucket List chock full of caramel apples, pumpkin seeds, crisp fires, candy corn, and football tailgates.

**My mother's birthday surprise:
"Johnny O."**

**Gramma Phyllis in her
signature casket outfit.**

July 19, 1997

The Last Easter Egg

My Dad and Natalie surprised us not
knowing we had our own surprise in store.

This family photo was taken by our dear friend Elizabeth Georgantas.

Pookie

Sami, Tyler and Mason

Owlivia

Owlivia in her final days in our neighborhood.

Crazy Colberts

Todd and Sami on a first visit
to Nantucket Island.

Todd delivered Pookie flowers on
her birthday in Nantucket.

Got any Kings?

Off to see Annie
with Gramma MaryLouise

Jack Colbert (left) and Bob Greenfield holding Tyler Greenfield (LSRHS '20) at the hospital shortly after his birth *Courtesy Photo*

In Jackson Hole, my Dad announced he would be known as "Pake Bitts," cancer-fighting cowboy, a character inspired by Annie Proulx's "Wyoming Stories."

Tyler Jack spending time with his grandfather in his last days.

Dale and Simba.

The arrival of a
new baby sister!

Todd & Sami
at the Colbert
Classic Golf Tournament.

Cousins.

When in doubt, use the cancer.

Pop, Mason, Todd and Tyler at one of Mason's football games.

Our goodbye visit for Ros and Aunt Pat.

Elon Homecoming with Tri-Sigma sisters.

Modeling snow pants.

The best ships are friendships.

College sorority days.

Gramma Phyllis's French Apple Pie

INGREDIENTS:

1 9-in pie crust

¾ C sugar

1 tsp. cinnamon

1 tsp. nutmeg

7 C peeled & sliced apples

1 ½ Tbsp Oleo (margarine)

Pie toppings:

½ C Oleo (margarine)

½ C brown sugar

1 C flour

METHOD:

Preheat the oven to 425 degrees.

Dot the bottom of the pie crust with Oleo.

Mix apples into a bowl of dry ingredients.

Sprinkle topping over pie and bake at 425 for 50-60 min.

Act Three: Cultivating Joy

Joybursts

Sipping coffee before the rest of your house wakes, freshly laundered sheets, a funny text from an old friend. It doesn't take much to brighten a mood for a moment. But how often do we stop and notice these small moments of joy?

During the pandemic, we spent time learning how to work safely in our offices while juggling our kids' hybrid school schedules and their new work-from-bedroom scenarios. Drained by Zooms and the guilt of additional screen time, the weeks became more difficult to manage. We worried about the mental health of our kids at home and those away in this new world of college. I needed to shift my own frustrations to a happier outlook.

Could highlighting what has brought us joy, help to build a happier outlook? Many of us have created other humans, so this should not be too much of a challenge. If a video made you laugh yesterday, today, spend a few minutes looking for other clips. If you enjoyed reading a book, maybe it's time to order a few more titles from your library? If you liked a song that came on your car radio, play that soundtrack at your desk. Once one friend posted how nice it was to buy flowers at the grocery store, many copied and shared. We can help each other. I'm challenging you to not only notice and share your happy moments but play them on repeat so you can build a happier day. Like Katy Perry reminds us, "after a hurricane, comes a rainbow." Baby, you're a firework, and it's time to create a joy explosion.

I suggested to two of my college friends that we text each other one moment of joy each day. "Share anything that makes you smile, or gives you a quick hit of joy," I explained. "Focus on yourself, not what you are doing to bring joy to others." My goal was to uncover what made us smile each day. I wondered how we could cultivate more happiness.

"Took a hot Epsom salt bath after dinner #joyburst" I sent to Bryson and Loren.

"Used a hair mask and blew out my hair even though I had no place to go," my friend Bryson shared.

118

"Met a friend for a run #joyburst," I texted.

"Listened to Oprah's podcast on a slow walk #joyburst" Loren sent us both.

"Eating my lunch outside without my phone," I sent.

Our bursts of joy became contagious. I turned off my alarm clock, remembering that Bryson enjoyed sleeping in the day before. I searched for a spa playlist which gave Loren a #joyburst the day prior. Todd asked me about their joy bursts at dinner and shared his own. If my day was gloomy, I found myself trying to find a reason to smile and share. The quest for joy bursts distracted me from my gloom. We shared photos of recipes, podcasts, quotes and songs. The more focus we shined on our joy, the brighter these moments became.

When our boys were small, we read the book "Alexander and the Terrible, Horrible, No Good, Very Bad Day," and laughed over how miserable he was. The more Alexander stomped around complaining, the worse his day seemed to get. Gloom breeds doom.

By changing our mindsets to search for good moments, we can find more reasons to smile. We don't need grand celebrations or adventures; we just need little everyday sparks to feel more joy. A text from a friend, watching a movie with your child, a warm bath at the end of the day. Simple moments bring joy and when added up, brighten our day. But it is up to us to search for these moments and savor them.

If you have been struggling to find joy lately, do not give up hope. Your search might take longer or be more difficult, but I bet you can find a little something to make you smile. On days when I can't find anything, I look to my friends to see what is making them happier and try to duplicate it for myself. That is why sharing your joy is so important-- you never know who might need inspiration at that moment.

I give my family books in their Christmas stockings, even though the books sit on their nightstands and often go unread. I have faith that eventually, someone will be inspired to read one of them. It hasn't happened yet, but I cling to hope. I have given them journals as well, trusting that they will use them when the time is right.

In early 2020, I started getting up earlier to add time to read and write in my journal. This simple tweak to my schedule has given me a few moments for myself to start my day in a positive mindset. On the weekends, Todd joins me with his iced coffee and laptop. It is a nice change of pace from our busy weekdays.

As I was writing this piece about joybursts, I looked over at Todd and noticed he was reading the book I gave him for Christmas, with our dog Simba warming his feet. That joy burst smacked me right in the face.

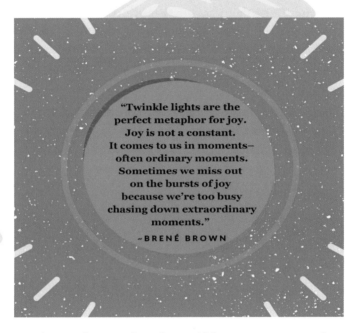

"Twinkle lights are the perfect metaphor for joy. Joy is not a constant. It comes to us in moments—often ordinary moments. Sometimes we miss out on the bursts of joy because we're too busy chasing down extraordinary moments."

~BRENÉ BROWN

During the pandemic, I found myself drowning in a sea of negativity. Having a son whose senior year of high school and freshman year of college was ruined by a lack of traditions, closure, and historic rites of passage. All the things you experience as you move through your teenage years were watered down by a worldwide virus. His brother experienced his own loss of social interactions, the joy of playing sports, and struggling to learn from a teacher on a screen. I chose the winter pre-pandemic to start a new full-time job, lured by worldwide travel and working at an inspiring all-girls school. I chose the exact environment, next to hospitals, that would be the most trying.

I challenged my friends to join me in recording daily moments of joy, or "joy bursts." I threw out the challenge in my *On the Sunnyside* column, suggesting that friends join me in sharing one moment each day for the month of February. I hoped a few would jump on board, but I also expected resistance. Many friends try to stay off social media, afraid of the time-suck. As much as I enjoy time off screens, I appreciate the connections with friends now more than ever. It cannot compare to in-person, but often a post will spur a real phone call or a walk with a friend.

These days, it doesn't take much to brighten our moods. Flowers bought while grocery shopping, listening to an old favorite song, a hot bath at the end of a long day. But how often do we stop and notice these moments of joy?

February 1st began with close friends posting their coffee before their kids woke up, flowers they bought themselves, exercise classes they sweat through. The #joyburst picked up traction and I created a Facebook group to give people a place to share. I watched my friends invite their own circles and inspire one another, celebrating their joys.

Seven days in was Super Bowl Sunday. A tough time for many who look forward to that celebration with friends. I reached out to my friend Keri and she helped me buy a ring-light. I needed to find the courage to create a video to reach more people. Too many friends are not patient enough to read about #joybursts, and I worried about the ones who weren't making time for their own happiness. Thinking about a simple joy makes you feel grounded in this crazy world. Sharing it inspires others to do the same.

"I took off the afternoon to go skiing- it was a huge joy burst!" A friend shouts to me across a busy parking lot in town.

"Thank you for giving people something positive to focus on," reads the note that is placed in my mailbox.

I knew people were hurting but did not fully understand how disconnected many were feeling. For some that is building connections, for some this is creating a positive routine, and building self-esteem and resilience. As we approach the year anniversary of the pandemic my hope is that we continue to share little moments of joy, and soak up all of their magic.

After a year of recording other people's #joybursts, I have compiled a list of the easiest ones to duplicate. My hope is that our sons and our grandchildren will read this collection of ways other people found joy, learned to savor it, and share in the happiness benefits. Once you find your joy, spreading it can be beneficial to growing it.

1. Buy yourself flowers.

2. Take a bath with detoxing Epsom salts.

3. Watch a funny movie.

4. Take a twenty-minute power nap.

5. Enjoy a cup of coffee before your house wakes up.

6. Snuggle with your dog.

7. Bake bread.

8. Bake cookies and sneak a spoonful of batter.

9. Take out a book from your local library.

10. Take a book to the beach.

11. Leave sand in the spine of your library book for the next person to find.

12. Scroll through the photos on your phone.

13. Text a photo to a friend to remind them of a fun time together.

14. Listen to a new playlist.

15. Text a song to a friend.

16. Create a playlist and share it with a friend.

17. Fill a bird feeder and watch your visitors fly in for a snack.

18. Try a new exercise class.

19. Teach a friend a new move you learned in the exercise class.

20. Use your wedding china for an everyday meal.

21. Use your crystal glasses.

22. Read a book in the afternoon. Fire and wine are optional.

23. Celebrate the day you met, got engaged, AND your wedding anniversary.

24. Plan a trip far in advance and enjoy the anticipation.

25. Buy your dog a sweater and share a photo with friends.

26. Get up to watch the sunrise.

27. Sit outside to watch the sunset.

28. Treat yourself to an ice cream cone.

29. Write in a journal.

30. Send someone a funny card.

31. Sit down and watch your child play.

32. Go for a walk outside.

33. Write a letter.

34. Facetime a family member or friend.

35. Brush your dog.

36. Dance to fun music.

You have the power to make yourself a little happier by noticing your joy bursts and playing them on repeat. If you like a song, you don't listen to it only once. If you like a beer, you order it again. Look back in the past week to see what brought you joy and repeat. These sparks will ignite instant happy feelings.

In order to harness joy's power, we need to find it, savor it, and share our joy with others. Allow me to clarify for those confused readers who may be foodies. You want to go out to dinner, and you may have heard about a new restaurant to try. You get a table and the cocktail is bubbly, the decor welcoming, and the meal is delicious. You snap a photo of your plate or your date, highlighting what is bringing you joy at that moment. "You should try this spot," you text a friend or post! This reinforces your positive feelings and shares it with a friend, who might be inspired to try the same spot or something similar. You receive replies or comments and each time it is another jolt of joy as you help others. "Ooh, I need to try that!" "Yay, we just went out to dinner too!" "I am going to try that next week!" You become grateful for the experience and the joy ripples.

SHARE YOUR JOY AND IT WILL SPREAD AND GROW.

The Recap

"What a great group!" my dad would exclaim when we were together with friends. Instantly his audience would beam up at him and sit a little taller. As soon as Dad belted that out, we would pause to savor the moment. We would be gathered around a table, or teeing off at a golf course, or setting up a beach barbeque. It didn't matter where we were, it reminded us to appreciate our surroundings.

I didn't realize it at the time, but as I research happiness, I am learning about the power of "savoring the moment." Savoring is gratitude's big sister, and the combo is scientifically proven to increase happiness. Savoring is the simple act of stepping out of your experience to appreciate it as it is happening. One of the easiest ways to enjoy the moment you are in is to take a picture. There have been MANY horrible days during this quarantine, but if you can stop and breathe in the good times when they come, you can shift your mindset.

Our family's favorite activity is the recap. We love to gather the day after a holiday or event to discuss the highs and lows. Sometimes we retell funny stories from the event and other times we might complain about a rude relative or food we didn't enjoy. We give more attention to the good moments, the stories get funnier, we remember the food tasting better, and the memories are a little shinier. It helps to recap with other people who can share their experiences through a different lens. An annoying interaction with someone can be flipped into a comical experience. Photos from the event help re-frame memories and enable us to share joy.

As I read about happiness, I learned about the power of "savoring the moment." Savoring is gratitude's BFF, and the combo is scientifically proven to increase happiness. It is the simple act of stepping out of your experience to appreciate as it is happening around you. One of the easiest ways to enjoy the moment you are in is to take a photo. You not only literally have to stop and focus, but you have photos to look back on the following day, week, or whenever you choose. Screens get a bad rap; the fact that we have the ability to text a photo from the palm of our hand is remarkable.

After I tuck my phone in for the night, I get into bed and recap the events of the day to find a few things that I appreciated. When I crawl into bed and recap the events of the day, I look for a few things that I appreciated. Sometimes I read the previous entries in my journal to remind myself of good times, especially if I'm having a tough week. Those recaps become fuel to power me forward. At times, I look through the roll of pictures on my phone, reflecting on the moments that stood out in some particular way to me and that I wanted to capture on film; a cute dog, a quote I took a screenshot of, or a meal that was so good, I wanted to save it. I force myself to write down three moments of gratitude from the day. Sometimes I read the previous entries in my journal to remind myself of good times if I am having a tough week, and those recaps become fuel to power me forward. I often need to look back at my camera roll to remind myself of a picture I took of my dog, a quote I shared, or a meal I enjoyed.

At the beginning of a new year, it is customary to look ahead and create goals and plans for the future. Before I take a step forward, I find it helpful to recap the previous year. Scrolling through my phone I am reminded not of the big splashy moments, but the little hits of joy throughout my week. An ice cream cone I enjoyed, a hike I took, a book I loved and sent to a friend. It is one of the reasons I like to share on social media. Those bursts scattered in my feed remind me of the good things I have experienced and give me hope for the year ahead.

STOPPING TO NOTICE WHAT GIVES YOU A BURST OF JOY WILL REMIND YOU TO CULTIVATE MORE SUNSHINE INTO YOUR DAY!

Got Any Kings?

Go Fish has been my favorite card game since I was little. I love the simplicity of the activity; no complicated rules to follow. You ask, you offer, you trade. The person with the most matches wins and you start another round. Isn't it ironic how this game actually works in real life? You ask for ideas, you share yours, you trade experiences, and in this case, everyone wins.

When I am exploring a place to visit or experience, I ask around to see who can offer suggestions. I love going "fishing" for new places to see, shows to watch or books to devour. I trade my recaps for new ideas.

Years ago my friend Caty shared that she kept details on her vacations in a travel journal. We were planning a family trip to Arizona and her notes provided me with great recommendations for places to see, stay, and eat. I duplicated her trip to Key West and passed along her ideas for Costa Rica to my brother. Knowing that a friend explored the spot prior to our arrival eased my anxiety.

To kick-off the summer, we took our family down to South Carolina. Charleston was on my "adventure list," and my youngest wanted to begin his college search in the south. Traveling to an area where we didn't have friends or family would ensure that we would have quality time together.

If you have teenagers, you know that "forced family fun" is not always met with enthusiasm. You may have seen Jennifer Garner's movies about parents who spent twenty-four hours saying "yes" to everything their children suggested. After a year of saying no to going out without masks, no to large gatherings, and just a lot of "no's" all around, we needed a "yes trip." Our version was to embrace spontaneity by following our son's recommendations, trying new foods, staying out later, and not controlling our vacation schedule. Our favorite activity was learning how to drive jet skis around the surrounding islands together.

Not all games are played with a group. When I am struggling to shift into a positive mood, I play mind solitaire. I use photos or quotes to help me to pause, reframe and taste the moment. In her podcast, Yale Professor Laurie Santos shares that you can increase joy by ruminating over the good parts of the experience before, during, or after. This is called savoring, which is the "act of mindfully attending to the experience of pleasure." You can also enjoy the moment by soaking up someone else's joy. My dad did an excellent job of this by asking "Does it get any better than this?" when we were together at a barbeque, on a beach walk, or enjoying coffee on his porch. Suddenly breakfast would taste better, the view got brighter, and the conversation livelier.

By displaying vacation photos throughout our home and giving gifts I have purchased on the trip or ordered online after we returned, I continue to savor. Hats or t-shirts from a favorite local spot, a cookbook from a yummy restaurant, or a candle whose scent reminds us of the adventure and intensifies the memories. I post pictures of our family vacation to inspire others to "trade" with me. Once I share my own journey, I can collect ideas for future trips and discover new places to explore. I create a dream list of future adventures which I keep in my daily sight. It is a game that gives me such joy.

The Joy of Travel

Planning vacations is my love language. I love talking about where we should go, who we should go with, and booking it far in advance to have a buoy to keep myself happily floating. Not only does having a trip on my calendar deliver hits of joy before I go away, but there are many bursts that occur during and after an adventure. There was a point last year when airlines dropped prices, we got vaccinated and were hopeful about travel going "back to normal," and we planned a Christmas trip with my extended family.

Unfortunately, there are many joy killers when people around you question your choice to travel. "Don't you have college to pay for?" "Haven't you taken a lot of trips this year?" Or my favorite: "Must be nice to be able to spend money frivolously." If you ask your wanderlust buddies, I am sure they can share a few zingers they have received. Many don't realize the additional benefits outside of the time to decompress, and in times like these, a trip could be the happiness boost you need. Here is my list of travel-planning joybursts to inspire your own:

1. **Planning a vacation helps fine-tune your decision-making skills.** With so many places recommended on the internet or from friends, you have to balance top interests with a budget, time, and physical ability to cram it all in.

2. **You improve your research skills.** While my husband Todd heads to TripAdvisor to check out excursions and plan our play, I like to scan Pinterest for the best dining and shopping. Now that our boys are older, they will find activities for us on the internet, making planning a collaborative effort.

3. **We recap the trip in a travel journal.** This helps us remember where we ate, played, and stayed so we can recommend spots to friends. It also allows us to learn from our mistakes. "Bring extra pens and cash," I wrote after our trip to St. Lucia. I am impatient if I have to wait for a pen as I complete endless forms in the airport so Todd stashes a few in the outside of our suitcases for the next adventure.

4. **Travel teaches you to communicate expectations.** While in St. Lucia, I wanted to hike to Pigeon Island, so my sister Sarah and I squeezed in a great walk and talk on our last morning. My brother wanted us to have a sibling dinner after his babies went to sleep. He explained his wishes to my mom so she would babysit. I asked Mason to take me on a quick

sail before we packed up and that activity kept my mind sailing the entire fourteen hours it took to travel home. No one should leave a place with regrets, and if you don't speak up, your bucket list item might not happen. I don't know anyone who vacations with mind readers.

5. **Taking pictures slows me down and allows me to literally focus on the beauty in front of me.** I love to frame photographs from vacations in our home to remind us of the adventure. Sharing the photos on social media encourages friends to comment and ask about the trip, causing a joy ripple effect.

6. **You learn more about friends and family when you go away with them.** Who likes breakfast, who enjoys exercising, who likes to nap, and who wants to be the "Julie McCoy, Ship Director" becomes evident. You also learn how to mediate between people as the activities may or may not line up with each other.

7. **The more you travel, the more organized you become, especially if you have to juggle COVID testing and vaccine verifications.** You will learn when to call in help to keep the experience enjoyable. We learned the joys of hiring a travel agent to plan our trip for fourteen family members. A travel agent can manage a wide range of ages, arrangements, and excursions, and always stay a step ahead of every travel change. The value of our travel agent was exceedingly evident when we had our own version of *Home Alone* and left our mother on Christmas morning at Logan airport. Our agent managed that crisis at a moment's notice, at the crack of dawn on Christmas, laughing all the way.

8. **Travel pushes you out of your own comfort zone and encourages you to flex your bravery muscle.** My mother is an anxious traveler, and will only travel with a companion. Her worst nightmare came true, but by the time she arrived on the island, she was proud of herself for getting out of her comfort zone.

9. **The text strings pre and post-trip, the sharing of photos, and the funny stories from the vacation are all bursts of joy.** You get closer to your travel buddies and it may inspire the group to plan another trip! It also gives you something to talk about with friends and colleagues when you return, making new connections.

10. **Finally, traveling makes you appreciate what you have.** While I was unpacking, my youngest son Mason came into my room and hugged me. "Thanks for making our travel look easy. I have never realized how many details you have to juggle." That one moment made me appreciate coming home with my core four.

The Magic Bean

I found a photo of when I was on the swim team, and I noticed that the spectators were watching the end of the pool. The race was over, yet I was still swimming. I was not a terrible swimmer but I was afraid of getting splashed. This was before contact lenses, and I thought goggles were clunky and dorky. It was difficult to be on the swim team since I couldn't dive. Like, at all.

I would stand on the starting block at the beginning of the race, trapped in my anxious mind, and simply fall into the pool. If you belly flop into the swim meet, there is no hope of catching up to the competition. My parents would yell at me after the swim meet. "You NEED to dive into the pool Sami. C'mon, just dive in. DIVE!" To their shock, this strategy did not push me to plunge into the water headfirst.

When I threatened to quit, my father tried a new strategy. "We will take you shopping to pick out a new Adidas tracksuit." I made it through a second season to get the matching pair of Nike sneakers. A new outfit didn't help me conquer my fear of diving, but I did look better in the team photo.

Some may consider the carrots he dangled to be a bribe, but I appreciated that he gave me something to look forward to in the end. I was never going to become a swim star, but getting exercise was good for me. They also hoped that joining the swim team would help me make new friends, but I failed at that goal as well.

My swim team memories help me today to pause and consider my fears. What's really going on when I don't dive in? When procrastinating on a project, I think, why am I standing on the starting block? Oftentimes, it is not the dive, but the fear of keeping my head above water. Many of us want to know what lies ahead and be guided into a new situation. We are all looking for a magic bean to get us up the beanstalk.

"You look amazing, how did you lose weight?" we ask, waiting to hear the secret.

"I moved more and put my fork down" is always the response.

"How do you have time to write?"

"I wake up earlier."

"How did you save money for that?"

"I cut back on my spending."

The magic formula we are all searching for is simple, but just like Jack, we have to accept that there is no magic beanstalk. Instead of beans, we CAN leave ourselves little breadcrumbs to keep us looking up and ahead. Meeting a friend for coffee, going out on a dinner date, planning a workout with a buddy, or booking a trip on the calendar. My friend Kate calls these "buoys," since they keep you afloat. They can be plans far in the distance, but having something positive to hold onto is proven to shift your mindset.

A childhood friend of my sister Natalie tracked me down earlier this spring. She had heard my father being quoted in a women's leadership event and thought I would appreciate hearing about it. I was not only touched by his words of wisdom, which I write about in my column, but also by the gift that this woman gave to me. I went on to reach out to the keynote speaker to let her know the impact her mention had on her audience. I didn't overthink it, I simply googled her and got in touch via email. It didn't take more than a few minutes of time, and I gained a wonderful connection.

The advice my father had given her was simply this: "Lead. Get out of your own way and dive right in."

Today, I make an effort to go head first off the starting block, and if the fear of water splashing on my face slows me down, I remind myself that I have a towel, and the ability to get out of the pool and dry myself off. I am also sure to keep a lot of buoys floating closely within reach. So I encourage you to go ahead and plunge right in and dive. DIVE.

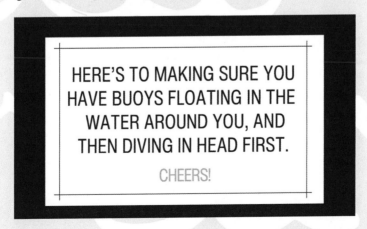

HERE'S TO MAKING SURE YOU HAVE BUOYS FLOATING IN THE WATER AROUND YOU, AND THEN DIVING IN HEAD FIRST.

CHEERS!

If These Walls Could Talk

When Saturday Night Fever comes on, I can't help but break into my old-school disco moves. 10,000 Maniacs brings me right back to college, and Neil Diamond has me falling in love with Todd all over again. No need for a DeLorean time machine, music has the power to transport me back.

My mother is a collector and would prefer to give away her treasures versus trashing them. Our boys enjoy the hunt of searching through the nooks and crannies of her home and discovering memorabilia. Early into the pandemic, we helped my mom clean out her garage and discovered her record collection. Promising to sort, organize and donate, Tyler brought my parent's record collection home. The memories came flooding back and we flipped through the albums. Seeing my first musical, Annie, with my grandmother in Boston. Going with my father to an evening showing of Grease, and then my dad brought home the record the next day. Creating dance performances to the Bee Gees with my cousins on Christmas. I began to play many of these songs and it was an instant mood-lifter.

Like many kids, our boys have spent more time in their bedrooms this year. Tyler used the records to decorate his walls, adding posters from his favorite movies. He decorated a wall in our basement with many of the album covers. As I walk by carrying groceries, I am reminded of the first concert I went to or my favorite song from junior high. Mason had Todd enlarge a photo of his favorite view so he could start and end his day with that spot in mind. I enlarged a photo from a vacation to Wyoming two years ago, and it is a beautiful sight as I get out of the shower each day.

I have a girlfriend who texts me songs that she knows I will like. When I told Tyler that I love the scene when Diane

Keaton writes to French music in Something's Gotta Give, he created a French playlist for me. In our weekly college Zoom, Loren built us a playlist from our sorority memories. Thanks to technology, music can be a quick way to brighten someone's day.

One of the downsides to this time is we cannot change our scenery with a vacation or getaway. We can fill our homes with music and make little changes to our walls that can help us reframe the space we are currently in.

I like to squeeze as much as I can out of vacations. I plan them ahead of time to give myself something to look forward to. I follow hashtags on Instagram, post questions about our destination on Facebook, solicit recommendations from friends, and tag locations on Pinterest to gather ideas. I soak up as much of the joy as I can by framing trip photos and memorabilia around our home as reminders of our adventures.

I spent time this spring creating a map of our favorite spots from our Jackson Hole trip last August, and as I painted, my crew added their own suggestions. It also inspired many dinner conversations on the adventures we shared last August.

Tired of spending so much time in their bedrooms this spring, the boys were inspired to add some flair to their space. These creative projects gave us all a spark of joy.

Don't let anyone burst your bubble.

Highs, Lows, and the
Joy in Between

**I found a journal I had written at thirteen
and it included a list of my likes and dislikes.**

*Likes: Reading during a snowstorm, in front of
a fire, snacks, steak, steamers, skating, and sledding.*

I assume it is a coincidence that my top "likes" begin with "S?" I enjoy all of those activities today, except rarely treat myself to these days unless the snowstorm falls on a Sunday, or I am celebrating with a surf-n-turf dinner out.

Slushy snow, changing my brother's diapers and wearing hats in winter top my dislike list. Hats do keep you much warmer, my mature self understands. Thankfully, my brother has also grown up and no longer needs help in that department. I am happy to have this sweet snapshot of insight into my thirteen-year-old mind.

At the beginning of the pandemic, we ate together every night. That joy wore off eventually. Tyler went to college, Mason had activities, and we began to eat solo; juggling virtual schedules.

In December, the band was back together again. We chatted away, sharing what we had missed since the last visit. Winter break was longer than usual and we got back into our routine of juggling and didn't always eat together. On one rare occasion when we were breaking bread at the same time, I suggested we share our "highs and lows."

When the boys were little, this was a great way for us to encourage small moments, and get a peek into their thoughts. What did they consider a low? What brought them joy? What did they have the courage to bring up? When we vacationed with my family, we would ask the group to share their highs and lows at the larger dinner table. The activity bridged the age gap and gave the group a new connection.

I love that our sons happily fall back into this routine without missing a beat. We learn about a struggle with a grade, frustration over a work issue, a connection with a teacher or coach. Sharing doesn't come easy in our house, so any crumbs I can gather are appreciated.

We are all tired and grumpy from the endless pandemic, and this season is cold and dark. I feel like a character on The Little House on the Prairie, preparing food and trying to get my chores done before sunset. I spend an hour making dinner, only to boomerang right back into the kitchen to clean up. We can talk ourselves into a circle of complaints and there are more lows than highs.

By bringing back the dinner game of "highs and lows," we learn what is making each person smile. It shapes the following day. If Todd's high was hearing that Mason took Simba on a walk, Mason might be motivated to repeat the performance. If Tyler's low was struggling over a paper he was writing, we might ask him to read it aloud. When my high is getting take-out delivered, we might go ahead and order take-out a second time that week; you can see the pattern here.

Taking a moment to share what makes you smile is not easy. If you read, watch or listen to something that lights you up, pass it along. Someone else might realize that they can duplicate it for their own pleasure.

"You bought yourself tulips instead of waiting for someone else to give them to you?" Bravo!

"You read a book in the afternoon on a Tuesday?" I can do that!

Playing in the snow instead of tackling laundry! That's allowed?

I have never heard of anyone complaining that they are tired from too much joy, or sick of smiling. This month, put yourself first and create more bursts of joy to power your day.

DO MORE OF ANYTHING THAT GIVES YOU LAUGHS AND DO NOT HIDE YOUR MAGIC!

Anxiety Baking

I struggled in math and science in school. I tend to read eighty percent of the directions, and I don't stress if I don't have all of the ingredients. For these reasons, I surprise people when I bake as often as I do.

"Oh no, talk to me, what happened?" My friend Kate uses my baking as an emotional barometer. She can gauge my anxiety level based on my baking activity. When my Mom's cancer came back in her mastectomy scar, Kate came to my house and found me covered in flour. If I am wound up or upset, the act of baking slows me down. As I mix sugar and eggs into a new form, I feel calm. Forced to focus my attention on measuring and reading a recipe, I get a break from my worry. When I pull the treat out of the oven, I have a sweet dessert to enjoy and share. Have you ever seen a grumpy person eating a gooey chocolate chip cookie warm from the oven? If someone pops into my kitchen and I can pass them a spoonful of oatmeal chip batter, I, too, am filled up. I bake to spread joy.

Ironically, I married a cookie monster. Todd loves to bake but is meticulous about measuring and following the recipe EXACTLY down to the suggestions of the order of ingredients into the bowl. C'mon, does it really matter if the sugar follows the flour or jumps in ahead of schedule? Todd also memorizes the recipe so he can make cookies any place we visit. Mason also bakes but he tends to create healthier versions of old favorites, while Tyler cooks savory dishes. That is how they give back joy to me. Nothing tastes sweeter than something made in my kitchen, but not cooked by me.

Greenfield Granola

4 cups oats (slow cooking)
1 1/2 cups sliced almonds
1/2 cup flax seeds
1/2 cup pepitas
1/2 cup walnuts
1/4 cup brown sugar
1/2 teaspoon salt
1/2 teaspoon cinnamon
1/4 cup coconut oil
1/2 cup honey
1 teaspoon vanilla

Preheat oven to 300 degrees.

Mix all dry items in a large bowl.

Warm honey, coconut oil and vanilla in a saucepan.

Pour over oat mixture until it coats.

Spread out on lined sheet pan (I use Silpat mats) and bake for 35 minutes.

As it cools, break up any clumps.

Add to glass canister and enjoy on top of yogurt with fruit!

Let your gut be your guide.

Pass the Face

I kicked off 2021 by taking an online improv class to conquer my fear of telling my stories on stage. In our class, we played a game called "Pass the Face," where you mirror the other person's emotions. You have no warning as to what their emotion will be, you simply have to catch whatever is thrown at you and make your face match theirs.

I play this game on a daily basis without warning. I walk in from work and when faced with a grumpy member of my family, I start to bitch and moan. My ride home from work may have been pleasant, but when greeted by unhappy people, I mirror their sadness. I try to fight it with a game of "Flip the Face," but quickly my positive attitude and face crumble.

"Make sure her head is held up. Slowly, one step at a time. Careeeeefffuuulll" my Mom smiled with gritted teeth as she coached me down the steep staircase.

"Your elbow needs to remain strong Sami to support her head."

When my new baby sister Sarah came home from the hospital, my impatient four- year old- self spent the morning waiting for her to grow up and play with me. Impatient that she was sleeping, I placed my newborn sister on a pillow and carried her downstairs to play. My mom heard me approaching and guided me with the calm demeanor of a bomb expert.

Since she smiled and seemed very proud of me, I confidently carried my new gift down the stairs. My Mom never lost eye contact and we played a winning game of Pass the Face.

I have since learned the power of the mind; she is a superhero. She holds the key to waking me up from a deep slumber, or the ability to question what her friend, my gut, is whispering. The mind can be guided, with some help, to deliver positive messages. My joy burst experiment is proof that you can cultivate a positive outlook by focusing on the small moments of happiness.

Fear is the brain's archnemesis and appears whenever the brain gets herself into a groove. Understanding its motives helps to decrease fear's power. As I reflect on my fears, I realize I don't put myself out there for fear of being a dork. I delete posts if they sound too dorky, or I think readers might judge me. I threw caution to the wind when I began publishing articles in the newspaper, but since I don't have to see people reading my writing, I am less afraid.

My fears are varied and range from irrational to logical – fear of dropping my phone into a porta-potty, fear of clowns, fear of birds flying inside, olives, dodgeball and volleyball, actually catching any ball near my face, diving, rejection, sharing my true passions, and failure.

The improv class was my attempt at conquering my fear of putting my creativity out there. It was a lot less scary on Zoom. I learned a lot about setting the stage and preparing before sharing my work in public. I learned that most people do not walk onto the stage and win over their audience immediately. They write sets, practice, and then perform. Rinse and repeat.

Whenever there is a creepy clown on screen, I run out of the room. For years, my family has been encouraging me to face my fear of clowns. Ever since I watched the horrific mime episode on Little House on the Prairie, I have been afraid of clowns. Clowns appear to be entertaining, yet a terrifying villain lurks underneath those creepy painted faces. My sons constantly ask me to watch clown-based horror movies with them, hoping it will cure my fear. My sister tried to talk me into a class where I would be chased by an actual clown, convinced it would help me overcome my fear of them.

Last week my son Mason tried a different approach to help me overcome this particular fear and asked me to watch the horror movie "It" with him. If you have teenagers, you know this rare gift I was given. The invitation would be revoked had I suggested a different choice. The crazy clown was scary, but not only did I survive, I felt a huge relief once the credits rolled. The proud look on Mason's face when we finished was a reward in itself. I called Tyler at college to share my accomplishment.

"I wish I could have seen your face!" he replied. I texted him a screen-shot of my beaming smile, happy that we can use technology to play Pass the Face.

SHARE YOUR JOY TO GIVE OTHER PEOPLE IDEAS ON HOW TO BE JOYFUL.

Perception is Everything

I can't go skiing because I don't have any equipment, I explained to my new boyfriend Todd. If you know my now-husband, you can imagine how excited he was about this idea.

"My family has tons of equipment that you can borrow! My Mom will pack us a lunch, and we can take a quick drive up to the mountains of New Hampshire."

I didn't want to burst Todd's excitement bubble but I had not skied since high school, and I was a pizza-pie-snow-plowing skier. I had a fear of heights and too many bad memories of my sister falling off ski lifts. As he chatted about the fun we were going to have, my anxious brain went into overdrive. But I did not want to ruin my "adventurous new girlfriend image," so I reluctantly agreed to go shop in his parent's basement.

If you are analyzing my anxiety at this point, I should explain that my in-laws are part superheroes. They all share some weird gene that produces an increased metabolism. No one in the family exercises to burn fat, they all need to burn off energy and ADD weight. Any sport they try, they excel at with the ease of an Olympic athlete. When I visit my mother-in-law in the spring, she will greet me in Linda Hamilton's arms which is extra impressive at eighty-one.

"Oh Sami, I have been rearranging the attic," she gushed. Mary Greenfield created at-home workouts before they were trendy.

Back to my story. I was greeted by my sister-in-law, the former ballerina, Jodi. "Help yourself to any of my ski stuff Sami," she graciously offered. I looked her up and down and knew I could only borrow her hat and earmuffs.

My mother-in-law steered me to the basement and went back to packing us a picnic lunch. Todd went off to the garage to wax our skis with his father, and I began sorting through the bins of clothing. To my delight, I slid into a pair of stylish black ski pants that fit me like a glove. I danced up the stairs and began shoop-shoop-shoopping into Greenfield's kitchen. This was going to be SO MUCH FUN!

"Hey Sami," Todd's older brother Chuck greeted me. Chuck resembled Thor and had an intimidating presence to match. I confidently waved, feeling like Suzie Chapstick.

"Why are you wearing my ski pants?" he asked me innocently. I turned ten shades of red.

Had I thought they were my sister-in-law's pants, I would have felt amazing, but now that they were my larger brother-in-law's, I was mortified. Confidence is a mindset and I was lucky to have such supportive in-laws.

Amen

Our family goes to church 4-5 times a year. It is challenging with the service only offered on Sundays at 9:30 a.m.. The only day we don't have to rush out the door. At the start of every year, it is always my biggest regret. While I complained when my mom dragged us to Sunday School each week, attending church also had a positive impact. I could be myself in the Youth Group and used the experience to write my college essay.

I kicked off the first weekend of 2020 with the bold intention that THIS would be the year we start going to church as a family. I was giddy over the idea that we might even go to an apres-church brunch! Yes, my expectations are often unrealistic. -)

That first weekend of January I began suggesting to my family that they be prepared to go to church. This meant reminding the boys when they were heading out Saturday night that they should set alarms and lay out clothes to get ready for the early morning. I now see this was hurting my cause. Of course, they both had late nights. I had to drag them out of deep sleep on Sunday at 8:45 a.m.. They went but grumbled complaints under their breath in our pew.

As I walked out of the sanctuary after not really enjoying the service, I bumped into a woman who lives near me and she thanked us for coming. I made a snide comment on how I was the only one who really enjoyed it – clearly, I felt like I needed to explain the frowns flanking me. "Next time come alone, I do it all the time since my teenagers don't always get up," Danielle cheerily explained. I walked away thinking "Ha- I am NOT coming to church alone! The whole point is to come as a FAMILY so our boys can have the same experience I had." My mom ended up eventually going alone to church and I thought that was heartbreaking.

Cut to today. I asked my family if we could go to church and the boys begged to sleep in since it is Super Bowl Sunday and they want to stay up later. I get it, they are going to have a busy night and sleep is very important in our house. So I dressed quickly, poured coffee into my travel mug (which is totally acceptable to bring into a church in 2020), and went solo. I am very social but it still makes me anxious to go to events alone.

"Good morning, I am so glad you came!" I was greeted by Danielle as soon as I walked into church. I told her this was my first time coming alone.

"Don your oxygen mask, Sami!"

Danielle was right, I did need to take care of myself first and bravely do what I feel is right for me. Today she was the bright light that I needed and she probably has no idea of her impact. Maybe that is how a lighthouse feels?

I loved the quiet meditative time that church gave me this morning. I sang loudly and no one rolled their eyes. I had time to think clearly and when ideas bubbled up, I pulled out a little notebook from my purse and jotted them down. It was a very peaceful hour. My mom used to explain that she liked the fact that church broke up her weekly routine and started off the next week in a new light. Some days she sang and other times she cried.

After church, I called my mom and told her that I finally understood why she went to church solo. Some experiences take twenty years to understand. This gives me faith that our boys might gain perspective in the future and that some of our lessons will sink in. I will shine brightly and help them find their way.

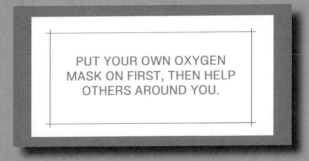

PUT YOUR OWN OXYGEN
MASK ON FIRST, THEN HELP
OTHERS AROUND YOU.

Let's Be Friends

As a young mother in a new town, I desperately wanted to make new mom friends. We moved to Sudbury when Tyler was two years old. I felt very isolated once pregnant with Mason. Sitting on a bench at the park, I would smile at other moms in hopes that we would strike up a conversation and become friends. I was invited to playgroups with my boys in tow, talking about sleep schedules, eating habits, and other new-mom-small talk. I invited a few of the moms over to decorate Christmas cookies the following week. I cleaned our house, baked cookies, and chilled drink boxes.

The night before my guests were to arrive, I went to a Christmas party and had a bit too much to drink. I was gnawing on a bagel and forcing down ginger ale to soothe my upset stomach as my guests showed up. Once the mom brigade had their coffee and the kids were deep into the sprinkles, I slipped into the bathroom to get sick. "Please get me through this party so I can go back to bed," I prayed into the bathroom mirror.

As I opened the bathroom door, Kate was standing at the door. "Sorry, I am super hungover and this Martha Stewart event is putting me over the edge," I explained.

Hugging me, Kate laughed and said, "We are going to be best friends." She explained how she nervously wore her cowboy boots to convince me she was cool.

Eighteen years later, we listen to our four children laughing together and I am grateful to Kate for cultivating their friendships. Her mother taught us the best toast of all: to friendships.

To tall ships, to small ships, to all the ships in the sea, but the best ships are friendships so here's to you and me.

CHEERS!

Sorority Life

Sorority Rush began with a round-robin of parties where you give a quick elevator speech to the members of the sorority. I pin on my name tag, grab a glass off the tray, and head into the crowd. Selling myself in two minutes isn't intimidating at this stage. I can be bubbly and charming in a morgue. My story improves with each round. My audience laughs, I ask the right questions, and I gain confidence with each lap through the chatty sorority sisters.

Looking back now, I am so grateful for the skills I gained during the sorority rush; skills I use each time I need to network in a large group. I learned how to sell myself in a short time. Greek life gets so much criticism on college campuses nationwide, but my experience left an indelible mark.

After getting accepted into my second-choice college, I was given a bid to my second-choice sorority. I didn't understand what the Greek system was all about, but it seemed like a ticket to a social life. In my freshman year, I only knew a few girls in my hall, and after I got lice, I kept my distance. Invitations were slid under our dorm door in the wee hours and we quickly opened the invite and ran up to the rush event. I remember jumping up and down with a bunch of new girls and not having a moment to dwell on my disappointment over being rejected. I was now cheering and hugging a group of women as we posed for photos with balloons and Greek letters like an SNL skit. I was thrown into a pledge class of twenty-two girls I had never seen before.

We were given daily chores that always had to be completed with a partner. We had to collaborate on many skits, dance routines, and self-written rap songs. Eight weeks of team-building exercises, community service activities, fundraising, and collaboration in a variety of projects connected us. We had to work together to figure out who could choreograph a dance routine, who could transform a bra into a headdress, who could rhyme, and who could draw cheerful posters. We leaned into each other's strengths and worked together to create something we were all proud of.

When I became president of our sorority, I learned how to lead meetings, become organized, and juggle philanthropies. Our sorority taught us about philanthropy and intramural sports teams. We created lip-sync dances for our Greek Week competitions and interviewed older sisters about their experiences. Above all, I gained a lifetime of friendships.

I may not remember my grocery list when I am at the store, but I can sing most of our sorority chants and will never forget the times I shared with this incredible group of women from the Tri-Sigma sorority at Elon University.

HERE'S TO JOINING A NEW CLUB, MEETING NEW FACES, MAKING NEW FRIENDS, AND CONNECTING IN A DIFFERENT POND. MAY YOU BE BRAVE ENOUGH TO SEE WHAT TYPE OF COMMUNITY YOU CAN CREATE.

CHEERS!

Choose Your Words

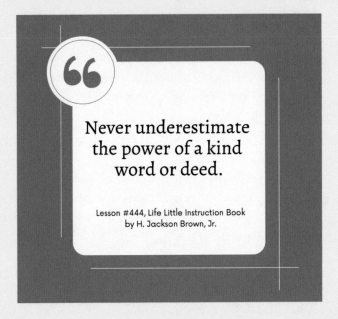

> 66
>
> Never underestimate the power of a kind word or deed.
>
> Lesson #444, Life Little Instruction Book
> by H. Jackson Brown, Jr.

"I've got you," the captain of the football team said to my son as he carried him off the field. Those three words relaxed him and later brought me such comfort as I was retold the story in the Emergency Room.

I heard from an old friend, "I had met this boy last fall and thought that we shared a spark."

"What ended things?"

"When I admitted I was falling for him, he told me that he respected me."

"Ick, are you his grandfather or love interest?" I asked.

One word, "respected," did so much damage.

"Thanks for doing the right thing," my son's boss replied when he texted in sick to work. Tyler had explained that after a strep test and COVID test, he still had a sore throat. He didn't want to let her down or jeopardize his job on his last week before heading back to college. Her reply was perfect and any guilt he felt evaporated.

"We are thinking about grabbing bagels and coffee and popping by for a visit if you guys are around? I text.

"Sure."

My enthusiasm deflates. Does that mean, "Sure, we'd love to see you?" Or "Sure, okay, if you want to." It's about as affirmative as "you look fine." "Sure" is on my list of words I don't like to use.

You've got this! Adventure, imagine powerful, brave, superior, shine, glow, wonder, smile, and joy. These are some of the words that jump-start my morning. I head to my coffee pot, ready to flip my pancake after hearing or reading these power verbs.

When my father was really annoyed, he started his lectures with, "with all due respect my friend" and nothing sweet ever followed. He was not your friend; he wanted to reprimand you and drive his point home.

"I'm calling to schedule an episiotomy." The nurse on the other line could not contain her laughter. My friend's husband asked, "I guess I need you to explain the name of the surgery that I'm looking for, and I expect you're going to be telling this story at cocktail parties?"

A friend of mine keeps an angry folder, after she writes an email when she is upset, she slides it into the folder for twenty-four hours and allows it to marinate. She then reads it the next day and decides if she still wants to send the message. She understands that she might need to change a few words in the light of a new day.

We tell toddlers "to use your words" as they are learning to speak. We often overlook the fact that the things we tell ourselves aren't always positive. I love writing because of the power that words hold. They can inspire, uplift, and motivate. They can express love or deliver joy to the recipient. Choose your words wisely.

Bubbles

My sister Sarah lay next to me, giggling as our Mom whispered instructions. Eyes closed, my hands over my belly, I tried to stay still and keep my Dannon coffee yogurt snack inside.

"Imagine an egg cracks on your head and is rolling down your neck," she guided.

"Gross," Sarah whispers beside me.

"Now the egg has turned to water and is slowly pouring down your shoulders. Breathe as it rolls down your arms," apparently she could hear us?

"Think of anything that is bothering you and let it roll with the streams down your body. Push it along with your breath."

I wish I could remember what I was worried about at eleven years old. My mom thanked us for being her guinea pigs and began setting up easels with graphic posters of dilated cervixes. We shuffled out of our living room as pregnant women were ushered in for their Lamaze class. I have used my mom's lesson when I have struggled to fall asleep.

Breathing is a skill we practice while exercising, stretching, or as you bring a little person into the world. When we are angry, anxious, or stressed, we forget its power and instead hold our breath. Fine-tuning the art of slowing down and exhaling can help us prepare for the uncertain future.

As children, we are given pinwheels, and bottles of bubbles, and encouraged to blow dandelion seeds into the wind. Kids know how to find the joy of breathing. As we manage our stressful lives, joining them in the yard might be the best move we make.

PUT YOUR WORRIES IN A BUBBLE AND BLOW THEM INTO THE WIND.

When you blow a bubble,
it catches the light
and changes colors as
it floats in the sky.

If you look away,
you will miss its beauty.

Stop to notice
before it pops!

Find A Hobby

I watch my eldest as he dices the onion with the precision of a fine chef. He slices the limes into an artistic arrangement and sharpens and cleans each knife when he's finished. He wraps each mini hotdog into its crescent blanket, using a small knife to carve expressions into their fleshy faces. He does not give in to my pleas to get the appetizer into the oven as our Easter guests are moments from arrival. He is too absorbed in his creative flow.

I arrived home the following day to the sounds of our younger son gliding his fingers across the keys of my uncle's piano. He plays a few songs for a well-deserved study break. He watched a movie in school and quickly learned to play the theme song.

A few days after my father-in-law died, so did our dishwasher. While Todd was writing the eulogy to read at his father's funeral, he would take breaks to tinker with the dishwasher. When appliances in our home fail, Todd takes the entire machine apart and builds it back together again in order to diagnose the problem. When Tyler's friend recently texted that he wanted to install a punching bag in his garage, Todd drove right over. Mapping out the design plan and the multiple trips to Home Depot, fueled his fire. It is one of the reasons that Todd enjoys helping others. He finds joy in rebuilding broken things.

For me, hobbies are a distraction or a useful break from a busy day. I'm a child of the '70s and grew up surrounded by women with hobbies. My mother sewed our Halloween costumes and prom dresses, my great aunt made Barbie clothes, my grandmother painted trays, decorative bags, and boxes, and took classes to make us porcelain dolls. My parents took cooking classes and disco dance lessons with their friends. They weren't expected to turn these interests into businesses or market their talents as side hustles. They weren't judged that taking disco lessons would take away from time spent on their responsibilities or work. We all understand that it only helped fuel their creative spirit within.

I grabbed a glue stick and created a scrapbook of the newspaper articles I have published. I take photos constantly on a hike, a run, or when we gather with friends and family. Transforming these photos into artwork for our home, posts on social media or albums brings me such joy. Walking by a scene from a past vacation transports me right back to the fun memory.

Hobbies do not need to lead to a business venture or take away from time spent working. They can be simple escapes or compliments to our busy lives. I think we can learn from our childhoods and welcome back hobby time.

Sleepless in Sudbury

Polishing it up so it would be extra sparkly, I dropped my tooth down the drain. Jesse remained calm and suggested that I write her a note. We worked on it together and slid my dear-tooth-fairy explanation letter under my pillow. We whispered from one bunk to the next. "What if she flies away and doesn't even see my note?" "What if she knows there isn't a tooth, so she doesn't go under my pillow?" My anxiety increased. I had been waiting all summer for this tooth to fall out and feared that I had jinxed myself by agreeing to this sleepover at Jesse's.

"What do you think she looks like?" I giggled as we lay in our twin beds imagining what the Tooth Fairy looked like. Jesse and I went back and forth describing our own versions of our heroine. We laughed over Jesse's image of a tight tutu-wearing older woman, and mine of a flinty Tinkerbell clone who was tight with the Easter Bunny. We eventually drifted off to sleep, forgetting about my huge mistake.

Sarah and I giggled nervously as we continued to bump toes, laying on our backs on the carpet. We stretched as she suggested and stifled our laughter over the large poster of a dilated vagina that is propped next to our mother. She forced us to join her Lamaze class to learn relaxation techniques but I remember us being too silly to focus. "An egg cracks on your head and you feel the yolk running down your face." Our mother's encouraged in a deep monotone to relax us as well as the pregnant women in our living room.

I try this exercise now when I lie awake overthinking. Like many women my age, I have trouble sleeping through the night. Instead of getting frustrated that I am awake and losing precious shut-eye, I replay these vignettes in my mind. These memories are the bedtime stories that lull me back to sleep.

"Sleep when the baby sleeps," was the first instruction we received as new parents. Those directions haunted us as we felt our chores increase and the time to complete them evaporate. A few months into having our first son, I realized that without naps, I couldn't make it through the evening to care for my child. In college, we stayed up too late, then had to power through morning classes the next day. An afternoon nap was key for social survival.

When our boys were toddlers, we would watch cartoons with them and I would sneak in a power nap. The boys were so engrossed in the excitement over watching a show that they didn't notice my eyes closed. Growing up, my parents had very active social lives, and they were big fans of the afternoon power nap. My Dad would pack multiple activities into his weekend, and a short nappetizer while watching golf on TV was his signature move. My mother preferred the after-dinner-mouth-agape-nap, which allowed her to stay up later to chat with any night owls. This came in handy the summer Tyler spent with her on Nantucket, since she would meet him in the kitchen after his night shift to catch up with him.

Today a nap is a luxury. If I have extra time, I love to sink into an afternoon slumber and prefer that as a way to catch up on my depleted sleep. A nap is my favorite part of a day at the beach, with the ocean or nearby music lulling me to sleep.

I have learned a lot about myself as I have aged on what brings me joy. Replaying my memories when I lie awake and a power nap makes that list. I plan to take a lesson from our dog Simba who naps with wild abandon after zipping around the yard.

She believed she could,
but she was really tired,
so she took a nap

Then she DID.

Be the Light

My oldest son Tyler hangs Christmas lights around his college dorm. My husband added lights inside of our porch creating the ambiance of a patio restaurant. Shining light on these dark areas inspired me to choose "light" for my word of the year.

Breathe was my word, then faith, followed by light. See a pattern? My words make more sense upon reflection. Faith reminded me last year to breathe and focus on being patient. I had to teach myself to trust that it would all work out.

2020 kicked off with a focus on connecting with friends virtually, and a pledge to guide friends towards funny times, reminding them of the pasts we have shared. At work, I shared the good around me and reminded those within the community of the positive steps the school was taking. I worked on my insides and helped turn on my Heart Light. I began sharing a bi-monthly column and burned bright. I chose Hope for 2021, and I have shared my hopeful thoughts and dreams. Hope to fuel us forward and keep us strolling in the right direction. Like a lighthouse, I hope to bring more light into other people's lives as they weather their storms.

Helping the Helpers

When Todd injured his foot, our friend Dylan appeared on our doorstep with a bucket of signature IPA beers and a bottle of my favorite wine. Dylan was aware of how just a small gesture of kindness could turn our moods around.

"I'm putting together a fundraising team for the Best Buddies ride," Todd expressed to Dylan. "Happy to help" was Dylan's immediate response. He didn't burden Todd with the business trip he had to rearrange, kid's activities he had to juggle, or his failing health. He met his fundraising goal, he conquered the 100-mile bike ride, and he joined the team at the finish line for a celebratory lobster dinner, albeit tired and sore but without one complaint. Dylan was that guy who was always willing to help. He seemed to find the reason to say 'yes' to your suggestion, versus his many well-justified reasons to say 'no'. He would agree to anything on the spot and then go figure out how to make it happen. He was truly an amazing role model.

When I started teaching a 5:30 a.m. spin class, Dylan was the first person to sign-up and attend. To be truthful, he hated my spin class, complaining that it couldn't measure up to an outdoor ride but he faithfully attended in support and gave me music requests to make it more enjoyable. He eventually convinced others to join, which led to them doing a CrossFit class for years to come. In that same year, I joined the *Goodnow Library Foundation* and he offered to help me in my new fundraising role, providing his experience and insight from his time on the *YMCA Board* in Connecticut. Dylan believed in the power of community and wrote our first appeal letter urging our town to support the library. His creative efforts were successful and it started an annual tradition that continues today. He knew how to ask for support.

It is *hard to help the helpers*. Dylan was battling a terminal illness that involved so many ups and downs and many of us struggled to find a way to support the man who lived much of his life helping others. His friends and family visited from all over to give him one last laugh and hug, which in hindsight turned out to be the best way to help the helper in his final chapter. We all know people who leave us too early, but lending them support can give us a jolt of good feelings, and that can be helpful to all.

Robert's Best

"Hello, I wanted to let you know that I got your note and am ready to sell my house. If you want to come by and see it before it goes on the market, you can come over on Sunday."

It took three years for Judy to call me after I put a note in her mailbox. We had three friends who lived on the street and loved the nostalgic feel of her neighborhood. Runners and dog walkers cut through the street, and kids played or rode outside reminding us of our own childhoods. Judy's was the only house that needed updating, which meant that Todd and I could afford it. Since it wasn't for sale, I tucked a note in her mailbox and didn't get a response for three years.

"Clearly this is a huge project that we DO NOT NEED."

"Oh, it has soooo much potential. I love it!"

We stood on the front lawn after our tour and I have never felt further apart from Todd. Our friends gave us the neighborhood sales pitch and I became more convinced that this was a great move for our family. Todd didn't even want to entertain the idea. We had spent seven years finishing our house and he was finally able to relax and enjoy his hard work. I made my case. I felt it in my core. This would be our home and we would make memories in this neighborhood. I pushed until we made an offer.

Middle School, High School, overnight camp, new puppies, the library, Todd's heel injury; so many experiences were intertwined with the families in our neighborhood. Our kids grew and fell into different cliques. We saw each other more frequently at town events and on fields and less on our streets.

During the pandemic lockdown, we started with waves, then drinks across the actual street, dog walks, another injury for Todd, firepits, tears, laughs, yard birthday celebrations, graduation car parades, tool swaps, book swaps, and a neighborhood of parents and kids closer than ever. Our teens had built new cliques as kids do in High School, but when we were all quarantined, they eventually started meeting in each other's yards. We projected movies onto our garage door, built fire pits, and rekindled their friendships from elementary school. Families gathered over remote, virtual, and hybrid learning plans, sharing frustrations and leaning on each other.

Some went off to college, younger kids created new carpools, and we welcome new families with potlucks on the shared cul-de-sac. We shared tools, referrals, and pet recommendations and connected intergenerationally. When our rescue owl became a town wide project, we welcomed new visitors to view the nest from our street. When I began my weekly newspaper column, neighbors would clip out the article and share supportive notes attached to their clippings.

Our mailbox filled with letters of gratitude, gifts of books, and owl ornaments, thanking me for sharing joy outside of our 'hood. The little mailbox proved to be the absolute best.

My Own Toy Story

My first toy was my Baby Alive Doll. Pretty creepy name for a doll. Her cheeks smelled like baby powder and were velveteen soft, ready to receive my kisses. Her mouth pouted and closed around her baby spoon. I carefully fed her the packaged oatmeal and changed her diapers after she pooped. By week two she was thrown out because my mom told me that she had gotten worms. Sounds pretty unlikely of a Fisher-Price toy, but then again, cleaning was never one of my mom's strengths.

I was given a pet fish to get over the loss of my baby. I named him "Ugly," and on day two, we ran out of activities to do together. I followed my mom's directions and only gave him a pinch of food each day. Until Thanksgiving. I justified that we were feasting, and so should he. Ugly never got to celebrate.

I was rewarded with a kitten, whom I named "Friday." Doesn't take a rocket scientist to figure out what day he moved in. No one can remember how long we had Friday since the trauma of her death overshadowed her experience. She ran away when we took her out of the car at the vet's parking lot. Not sure why she was traveling like a person, but let's not blame my mother for everything. Three weeks later, someone replied to our missing cat flier and a very skinny, frost-bitten Friday staggered into our house. My Mom laid her in front of the furnace, but Friday must have already cashed in eight previous lives. The poor unsuspecting babysitter helped my mom carry Friday out of the basement on a shovel. And that traumatic memory sealed my cat-hating fate.

At this point in my life, I found joy in a plastic, lifeless toy: Barbie. Not sure who gave me my first one, but once I met Barbie, my life became sparkly and magical. Birthdays and Christmases brought all the cars, vans, houses, campers, clothing, and additional family members to round out my Barbie collection.

"What's wrong?" I whisper in the dark. "You can tell me."

"I'm too embarrassed," my cousin Niki sniffled.

"It's okay, I understand, I won't make you feel like a baby," I reassured her from the top bunk.

"I get it. You want to play Barbies but you think we're too old. We can play Barbies and I promise not to tell anyone."

Nikki laughed through her tears. "I am homesick and I don't think I can sleep over," she confessed. My cousin started laughing hysterically.

Niki and I would have sleepovers and play Barbies under flashlights. We set up a village in my attic and would get lost in our own world for hours. One of the best days was when my babysitter, the youngest of four girls, gifted me her entire Barbie collection. The Barbie Dream Home, corvette, motorcycle, hair salon, and the ultimate: the Barbie camper. Niki and I creatively built homes and used my disc camera to photograph the dolls. We made miniature picture frames so Barbie and Ken could have their own memories on the walls of their home. My Aunt Judi did not appreciate our vision when she developed six rolls of Barbie and Ken photographs. We used my boom box to record interviews with Barbie and her friends. I am now realizing that Joanna and Chip may have stolen their ideas from us. Just maybe?

Barbie was a real go-getter who could do anything she wanted. She played by her own rules. If she didn't want to drag Skipper along, there were no parents to tell her otherwise. Barbie quickly slipped into a new costume if she wanted to change things up. I had her driving her Corvette in a wedding gown. Or wearing a leopard coat, over her pink pants, to pick up Ken for a weekend camping trip. She was a nurse one day, and a popstar the next.

My great-aunt made clothes for our dolls and I keep my favorite Barbie coat framed on my shelf. Over thirty-five years later it is a great reminder to play with the people who light us up.

Flashlights

My husband interviewed a young man recently for an accounting role at the company where he works. The young man sat upright, clean-shaven, wearing a well-pressed suit, poised and professional, but nervous as any new graduate would be at one of their first interviews. He recently graduated from the University of Massachusetts and was seeking an entry-level position.

"I see on your resume that you went to Waltham High School? Do you happen to know Mr. Rono?" Todd asked to help find common ground with the candidate. His reply was beyond heartfelt.

"I sit before you Todd, because of Mr. Rono. I never thought I would have the opportunity to say this, but Mr. Rono inspired me in economics and helped make me who I am today. He took our class on a field trip to Deloitte at which time I was enlightened to a career that I would eventually pursue. I worked hard to get into UMass, and now am proud to have graduated and be interviewing with you today."

Up to this point, this young man did not know that Mr. Rono is one of Todd's closest friends and that it was our brother-in-law who arranged the tour at Deloitte.

Later that evening, I re-watched the award-winning movie Coda. We had watched it earlier in the year but felt that it was worthy of another viewing. I have previously posted about my love for this film, and it has come up in many conversations with friends since, especially after winning an Oscar. I had forgotten about the influence of Mr. V., Ruby's choral teacher in the movie. I won't spoil the movie, but for those that have seen it, we know that Ruby would not have gotten to where she landed without Mr. V shining a light down upon her and making her believe in herself. It is evident that there is truly nothing more inspiring than the support and encouragement of a teacher.

Timing is everything, and this article should land at the time when parents are thinking of ways to show their appreciation for the amazing teachers their children have had this year. I do not need to remind any of you just how difficult the teaching profession has been over the last few years and how "Zoom" is a new four-letter word that they never signed up for. Teachers deserve the greatest respect and recognition and have been a guiding light for our children. Let's make an effort prior to summer, to not forget how much we all need these flashlights in our life.

BE GRATEFUL FOR THE HELPERS AND THOSE WHO SHINE LIGHT AROUND YOU.

WE CAN BE GUIDED BY THESE FLASHLIGHTS.

Savoring

"What a great group!" my dad would exclaim when we were together with friends. Instantly his audience would beam up at him and sit a little taller. As soon as Dad belted that out, we would pause to savor the moment. We would be gathered around a table, teeing off at a golf course, or setting up a beach barbeque. It didn't matter where we were, it reminded us to appreciate our surroundings.

I didn't realize it at the time, but as I research happiness, I am learning about the power of "savoring the moment." Savoring is gratitude's big sister, and the combo is scientifically proven to increase happiness. Savoring is the simple act of stepping out of your experience to appreciate it as it is happening. One of the easiest ways to enjoy the moment you are in is to take a picture. There have been MANY horrible days during this quarantine, but if you can stop and breathe in the good times when they come, you can shift your mindset.

This photo was taken on the day that Mason had broken his retainer, Todd had a third X-Ray to check for a possible bone infection, and Simba had to go to the Pet E.R. for a balance issue. Todd stopped working in the garage (you can see from his outfit), and convinced Mason that he could figure out how to cut his hair. You can tell that Mason is laughing along with Todd (and asking me not to take his picture in the pajama bottoms he has cut into shorts).

I could have focused on all that was broken that day, but instead, I stopped to savor this funny scene. And when my grandchildren ask us what it was like being quarantined in 2020, I will have something to share.

What a GREAT group.

RAISE YOUR GLASS

Is There No Place Like Home?

In *The Wizard of Oz*, Dorothy spent most of the film trying to find her way back home. If there is one thing I appreciated during the pandemic lockdown in 2019, it was learning that she was correct in feeling that there is no place like home.

Inspired by Dorothy, I closed my eyes and imagined what made our own home feel good. Was it having fresh flowers displayed? Cozy throws and a fire roaring? A bar cart stocked to mix a cocktail? A fun playlist humming in the background?

Growing up, we called my mom the tornado, and with four children and four pets, she left destruction in her wake. Our home was in sheer chaos and we have carried that into our own families. I wanted my own home to feel peaceful and provide a place for us all to recharge. Some years there was playdough stuck to our carpets, a highchair covered in food, or we were rushing in from a soccer game, or frantically searching for lost homework. But during the pandemic lockdown, we had time to get to know our home again.

I realized that I needed quiet space to think. Sometimes I would get that early in the morning, in a bath, or on an outdoor run. Since I did not have a commute, I needed to carve out other areas. Todd and I redecorated our porch and created a space to savor our coffee, gather with friends and family, and sip cocktails while the sunset. We made sure the chairs swiveled and were comfy for endless conversations. A true area to reconnect and recharge. We added a gas stove to our porch providing warmth and ambiance. When it snowed and we sat out there with the fire going, it felt like being inside a snow globe. As the sign that hangs on the wall, it truly is our "Happy Place."

Seeing no need for a formal living room, Todd and I decorated the room for music and working. We moved my desk to the window which enabled me to enjoy the natural light while working and keep an eye on our dog, *Simba*. I displayed my favorite children's books for inspiration, a cozy chair to change up my writing space, and plenty of journals and pens. Our sons were taking piano lessons on an electronic keyboard but they were struggling to practice and stay motivated. My uncle rescued our piano from a local church and it was not in the best shape, but it does play music. By strategically placing the piano in the boy's path, they would often stop to play a few tunes as they walked by. A sign from a local shop displayed the song from Mason's first performance at preschool. "I love you in the morning, and in the afternoon, I love you in the evening and underneath the moon." It is a great reminder of Mason singing that sweet song.

As a mom of teenagers, I spent a lot of time in the laundry room. Having it situated in the kitchen made it easier to manage. We added a gallery of photographs taken by our boys on their phones so they remain inspired to continue to capture and document small moments. Our mantle held a glass bottle of my grandfather's, our bookcase a wooden angel that my Grandmother made, we curled up under the blanket she knit, and my desk featured a tray, a candy dish, and a painted box that she gave us at Christmas. My in-progress needlepoint is in my grandmother's tote bag, and I have my mother's needlepoint collection framed as a reminder to get to the finish line. The story of my grandmother sharing her gift of homemade presents inspired my very first blog post.

Each morning, I see the golf ball that Todd gave me and the framed lyrics of the song he played when he proposed twenty-six years ago. Photographs are framed throughout the walls of our house to highlight the adventures we have shared. Savoring the memories of costly vacations decreases the sting of the expense.

When asked what brings us joy in our home, I do not list expensive furnishings or the actual house, but the little items that tell our story. It is a space that contains a collection of things we love, photos, and items from places we've traveled, and enables us to share our joys with our guests. Every room is an opportunity to highlight the memories we have created and display them for our guests.

After spending more time with her during the lockdown, I truly realize there is no place like home. If your home doesn't tell your story, now is a great time to write it.

Flip Your Pancake

I love the memories attached to old photographs. Once I proved I could care for my pet goldfish "Ugly," I was given a kitten who I named "Friday." It is obvious which day he joined our family. Friday brought me joy until he died a tragic death of frostbite. Memories of my mom yelling at the babysitter to help her try and nurse Friday back to health, the way we handled grief and emotions in the '70s, and my distance from future pet cats are funny if you share my dark sense of humor. Sharing photos is one of the ways I change my attitude when I am feeling down.

I often burn the first batch of pancakes I make. I am not known for my patience, so it is a pretty safe assumption that it is due to a failure to wait for the griddle to heat up. I have accepted my pancake failure and simply toss the first few into the trash and focus on the golden perfection of pancakes number three and four. Blueberries bursting at the seams, butter oozing down the stack, and a signature "dipping pool" of syrup accessorize my Instagram-worthy breakfast. Posting a photo helps me to savor my creation and inspires others to build their own pancake stack, or head to their nearest diner for breakfast.

My first thoughts after Alexa wakes me are often of my day ahead and the tasks that will follow. It takes an effort not to get dragged down by the burnt side of my day. When I arrive in the kitchen and see last night's dinner dishes that "needed to soak," my mood gets soggy. Owlivia, our pet rescue owlet, helped me each morning to "flip my pancake," or shift to the positive side of the situation.

During the two months when I was greeted in the kitchen with video footage of Owlivia, I could change my mindset and start my day with joy. My husband and I drank our coffee hunched over his phone like proud parents watching her midnight feedings. I would post to social media and immediately see the ripple of friends, relatives, co-workers, nurses, teachers, doctors, and children enjoying her growth.

"We are listening to their hoots as we fall asleep each night."

"I played the video for my kindergarten class and they were mesmerized."

"We gathered at the nurse's station and replayed the video so many times!"

We made new friends, connected with old ones, and watched relation-ships grow alongside her. When my motherly instincts kicked in, I relied on my social feed to share positive thoughts, prayers, and insights into her worrisome behavior. It was during a time when many of us were concerned for our own nests. Would our own children survive this time, would they fall, would they learn to fly after a year of lockdown, would they leave the nest? *Owlivia* gave us hope and a beautiful distraction from the crazy world around her tree. She gave us a positive connection that expanded across generations.

I will never forget what Owlivia looked like the day we met her. That little fluff ball with giant eyes looked like they were sewn on. The first time she smacked her beak into our camera was when she gobbled down a mouse in one bite, the way she watched her mama fly from the nest. The memories we have made this part a little easier to swallow. Having to let her go was difficult, but I am grateful we had the time to appreciate this little miracle. She taught us to thoughtfully observe animals in nature around us and reminded us that the gift is fleeting.

After this year, you may read many suggestions on how a pet can improve your mental health, but that term can be used loosely. A pet rock, a snail, a stuffed animal, or even a wild animal can immediately improve your day. At a time when many of us feel burnt, it is important to latch onto something to flip our mindset. Don't get discouraged if you have to toss out the first batch. Once you flip your pancake, you will be looking ahead at a full stack.

There are little daily rituals that can help shift your perspective:

1. If you want to find joy, get up a ½ hour before your family. Make coffee or tea and either bring it back to bed or savor it in your quiet kitchen.
2. Stroke your pet.
3. Give a loved one a long hug. Do not be the first to let go.
4. Listen to the birds.
5. Write a card to a friend.
6. Walk around your garden.
7. Watch the clouds go by or the sunset drop.
8. Star gaze.

CREATE BEFORE YOU CONSUME.

Gramma Phyllis's Blueberry Pie

INGREDIENTS:

1 9-inch pie crust (frozen is fine)

4 C fresh blueberries

1 C sugar

3 tbs. cornstarch

1 tbs. butter

½ tsp salt

½ C water

METHOD:

Fill cooked pie crust with 2 C blueberries.

Make sauce by cooking blueberries with sugar, cornstarch, salt and water over medium heat until thickened.

Remove from heat and stir in butter and cool.

Pour over berries, into the crust.

Chill until serving time and serve with real whipped cream.

Epilogue: Leaving a Legacy

Dance Like Nobody's Watching

"Oh, how I had missed my waist. After a year of wearing maternity clothes, and six months of breastfeeding, I happily cinched a belt around my waist. I practically skipped into Old Navy with my sister in tow, ready to load my arms with new pants and tops that would fit.

Sadly, every top I tried on wouldn't button closed, and the pants? Forget it. Clearly, these extra larges were mislabeled! They must be extra SMALL!

Or had I been Shallow Hal'd?

The truth is, if I hadn't stepped into that Old Navy, I'd have continued to walk around my house thinking I looked like a supermodel. I felt good, so I knew I had to look good.

Shallow Hal was the movie where Jack Black's character was hypnotized into seeing only the beauty in women. or maybe I was closer to Amy Schumer in I Feel Pretty? The premise is the same, you can trick your mind to only see the good and you will in fact feel better about yourself and those around you. if I had not gone shopping I would have continued to walk around my house thinking I looked like a supermodel.

A week later, my in-laws offered to babysit so Todd and I could enjoy New Year's Eve out with friends. I went to Target and bought a Gramma Phyllis signature gold blouse that not only fit, but emphasized my voluptuous new cleavage. I paired it with black maternity pants, and boots to heighten the overall look. You can imagine how sexy I was looking. I danced the night away, sneaking breaks to pump in the bathroom. At one point, I strutted by my friend Rob, hip-bumping him as I slid by.

"Hey Sami, he yelled over the loud music." I tossed my overgrown hair over my shoulder and turned back towards him.

"You are leaking." I looked down to find my blouse soaked in milk. I guess sometimes it is nice to stay in your own head.

Be Kind

While my friends may have a hard time believing it now, I was a painfully shy eleven-year-old. At that tender age, I was given a gift that would stay with me my whole life in the form of a school project.

Butterflies danced in my stomach as I stood with my classmates inside the Belmont Public Library, my Dorothy Hamill haircut pulled back in the ribbon barrettes I'd made in Girl Scouts. The librarian escorted us through the stacks, and there it is - *Susie and the Ballet Teacher* by Sami Colbert. I can still recall how I lit up seeing my book on the shelf, and know it was then I became inspired to use writing and drawing as a way of self-expression. I drew, I wrote diaries, I painted murals and I learned to share my stories.

When I went on a field trip to George's Island in fourth grade, I hung back with my teacher. They didn't assign you, buddies, back then, so off the bus, I would wander by myself. The boy who sat behind me in class, Jason Conti, came up to me on a path with his shiny new 110 camera. He ran around taking pictures of himself, the seaweed, the rocks, anything to get me to smile. We spent the field trip photographing the island and I quickly forgot that I was not with the other girls from our class. Jason's (aka Crazy Legs today) kindness left a mark. You truly never know who you can touch with a simple gesture.

Passed Down From Pookie

In honor of Mother's Day, I sent my mom a list of tips my mom has passed on that I appreciate today.

1. A hot bath at the end of the day. Light a candle, pour in some Epsom salts, grab a book and feel your negative thoughts flow down the drain. On Tuesdays, I bring a drink into the tub since that is always the day that I fall apart.

2. Baking homemade granola makes the house smell amazing and a sprinkle on yogurt is delightful. My mom - Pookie to her grandchildren - also likes to toss frozen meatballs and a jar of sauce into the crockpot with lots of basil and oregano. She claims "doctoring them up" gives the illusion of being homemade and again makes your kitchen smell delicious.

3. Keep a "gift closet." I keep a few books, candles, and wine so when I see a cute hostess gift, I buy it so I am prepared when we are invited to someplace. I appreciate that she taught me to be well-stocked.

4. A funny movie can shift your mood. Preferably one with Diane Keaton and/or directed by Nancy Meyers. Being home for eight weeks, I have turned to many of these in times of grumpiness and I can't help but laugh.

5. You can read multiple books at the same time. I keep a self-help book near my kitchen, a parenting book on a coffee table, and the novel I am reading at my bedside. I also tend to have an audiobook on my phone. I thought it was nuts when my mom carried a book in her purse and kept another one in her car. I now also enjoy reading different genres at different times of day.

6. Choice Night. Growing up, this was one of our favorite nights in the Colbert kitchen. As long as we made it ourselves, on "choice night," we could have anything we wanted for dinner. We learned to team up and cook for each other. I almost always made apple-baked chicken, while my sister Sarah whipped up yogurt sandwiches.

TO CREATING YOUR OWN TOOLBOX.

CHEERS!

Make Someone's Day

So much of our day is planned. Many of us live by schedules, lists, calendars, meetings, appointments, and to-do lists. Giving a gift is a little break into that routine, a surprise burst of love. Gifts do not have to be extravagant. A bouquet of flowers can brighten a gloomy mood, a thoughtful present of a book, a candle or something you picked out that simply says; "I was thinking of you."

It has been proven that spending money on someone else can make you happier. A study in Health Psychology found that "when given money to spend on others, participants experienced heightened feelings of social connection and lower levels of stress. "Spending smaller amounts, even just $5 does the trick," says the study author Ashley Whilians, PhD, a behavioral scientist at Harvard Business School. "Pick up a friend's coffee every once in a while, just for a burst of joy.

My mother liked to plan her gifts in advance, picking up things as she saw them and then keeping them in her "gift closet." When we had a birthday party to go to, or if we got an invite, she directed us to the closet where we could find birthday presents for kids of all ages, and housewarming presents if we were invited to stay over. It also helped my mother decrease the number of times that she had to run out to the store at the last minute, an everyday occurrence with four kids. I do keep a gift shelf with wrapping paper, gift bags, and a few of my favorite books. Think of something you have received and how it made you feel. Did you receive a card that made you giggle? Did you enjoy warm banana bread when your friend spontaneously stopped by your home?

Here are a few ways you can brighten someone's day for under $10:

1. Treat them to a coffee either in person or with an e-gift card.

2. Mail a funny card.

3. Buy a bouquet of tulips (be sure to tell them to add a penny to the water to keep them fresh).

4. Send a book that you enjoyed reading.

5. Give a candle to light their way.

6. Bake cookies, brownies, or banana bread, and slip them on their doorstep.

7. Deliver a bottle of wine to their home.

8. Visit them for a deep hug.

Is there something you can send today that would brighten someone else's mood?

When it comes to spreading joy, there is no time like the present.

Going on a Bear Hunt

It is a myth that women forget the pain of childbirth. We have not actually forgotten the pain, we have just replaced it with the memories of happiness that we experience upon holding our newborn baby. Scientists refer to it as the "Halo Effect" and it has been proven to change our perception of reality. It isn't that we are wearing rose-colored glasses; we are highlighting the joy of the new baby and giving less air time to the pain of the delivery. I think parents do the same thing when they describe the joys of getting their first child off to college. They focus on the planning and the adventure of finding a school that fits, and less on the actual delivery into their new home. I think the children's story: Going on a Bear Hunt prepared me for this.

In this beloved children's book, the family heads off on their journey to find a bear. They try to make it a fun game, but after many exercises, they learn that they can't go under it, or around it, they simply need to go through the squishy muddy parts to get to the end. Last fall, I asked my therapist how I could make the transition easier and less depressing. She simply told me that I need to go through it. I couldn't go around the sad parts, or over the painful ones, I simply had to wade through them. I found her advice helpful.

While I have felt heartbroken again this year with sending my second son off to college, the drop-off was easier the second time around. This time, I knew it would take time for everyone to adjust. I also realized that nothing is final and I don't have to stress because we've all learned how quickly things can change. The fun adventure was preparing, packing, getting his dorm room setup, checking out the campus, and eating at local hot spots. Now the muddy squishy part is not as much fun, but I imagine catching an actual bear isn't either.

Ironically, just as I was sending my oldest off to school, my sister-in-law was giving birth to my niece. My niece was over nine pounds but my sister-in-law gushed into the phone about how wonderful she felt and elated they both were about having sweet baby Jane. She and my brother are navigating the joy of living with a toddler and an infant. I won't give them any advice because they, too, need time to go through the mud and try and stay focused on the adventure of it all.

IF YOU HAVE BEEN
STRUGGLING
TO FIND JOY,
DO NOT GIVE UP.

YOUR SEARCH MIGHT
TAKE LONGER OR BE
MORE DIFFICULT,
BUT I BET YOU CAN
FIND A LITTLE
SOMETHING TO
MAKE YOU SMILE.

RAISE YOUR GLASS

Random Acts
of Kindness

She explained how she swaddled him tight and got him to take a bottle, and I gratefully fell into her deep embrace. It was after midnight and I was sure Melissa needed to get home to feed her own newborn baby boy. The following day started with discussions of who would speak at the funeral when we would hold it if we would wait for outer towners to fly in. At some point, a dress from Ann Taylor appeared on our doorstep, tags on and in my size. How did Cathy know I needed a funeral dress? Jennifer arrived with an overnight bag, and I protested, not wanting to take her away from her new husband. She sat with me as I cried in disbelief. She placed a plate of eggs and toast on my lap as I nursed my baby boy, and I gratefully swallowed each bite.

We greeted hundreds of guests as they came through the line of the wake.

"Oh, she's okay. We are fine. We'll all be ok," I comforted guests and reassured them that we were going to get through this tragedy. Our feet ached, our tummies growled, and my cousins helped me take breaks when my milk came in. My mom's friend Kathy whispered into my ear that we should drive over to their house once we were finished. Swollen-eyed and exhausted, we wrapped up the day with the odd tradition of standing by our father's casket.

Kathy greeted us as her husband Craig played the piano in their living room. Their elaborate table was set with candlelight, and fine china, and their children stood at attention like waitstaff. They served us a feast and we gobbled up every last bite. We laughed and cried as we shared stories of Sarah's dates making their appearances at the wake, and other awkward moments. The family waited on us like we were in a fancy restaurant while we reminisced about our Dad. We slept well on the eve of his funeral thanks to this very generous family. Twenty years later, these random acts of kindness are the moments I cannot forget.

After the first Sunnyside column I published, my friend Sue laminated the copy and I gave it to my father-in-law. A new friend Bethany, mailed me her extra copy with the sweetened note of encouragement. I received a handmade card with a package of decadent warming chocolate from a friend I have not seen since middle school. I am touched that she took the time to purchase, create, package, and send me this gift all the way from n Eureka, California.

Many think generosity comes from your wallet, but sharing your time, energy and words can make other people around you feel good. When you are surrounded by good people, you feel lighter. When you are the giver, you shine a little brighter. The "Giver's Glow," coined by Dr. Stephen G. Post who has researched this theory in his study at New York's Stony Brook University, shows that often it is better to give than receive. And a random act of kindness is an activity you can try any time.

We've Come So Far

The first time I heard my father cry was after the first plane crashed on 9-11. He called to tell me how worried he was for his staff as they were evacuating his building, and he encouraged me to do the same. When I go into Boston today and see the skyscraper he worked in, I am reminded of how much we have learned since then. If I could, I would send my Dad a text about the following things that would blow his mind.

1. Streaming services: he went to West Coast Video each Friday to rent a stack of movies. Netflix would blow his mind.

2. Smartphones: he loved his palm pilot but I'm sure that little pen would have gotten annoying by now.

3. Online shopping: he thought it was amazing to call Nordstroms to order shirts. It was also a bargain hunter and would have had fun hunting for deals.

4. Hot Yoga and the ability to watch an exercise class in the palm of his hand. My Dad was into any new exercise trend.

5. Cooking videos on Pinterest, Instagram, and TikTok. He loved planning a good dinner party and the ability to share his ideas with his own herd would make him very happy.

6. Digital music since all of his parties ended on a dance floor.

7. Tyler, Mason, Madelyn, Sophie, Jack, Jonathan, Jill, Koji, and Simba. The family was everything to him and he would be obsessed with how easily he could connect with everyone, even the dogs.

Can you create a list of what joy your loved one would have experienced since they passed? Collaborate with your family and laugh over the memories together and you might feel a little better about the time lost.

JOY MAKES YOU
STRONGER AND
HEALTHIER.

IF YOU SAY A
JOYBURST BEFORE
YOU GO TO SLEEP,
IT WILL HELP YOU
REST HAPPILY.

CHEERS!

Taming My Tongue

One of my goals in life has been to learn to bite my tongue. You can imagine how challenging this is since I like to share every thought that pops into my head. Then, teenagers happened and this goal moved to the top of the wish pile. I listened to many podcasts, read a few books, and gathered insight from friends who are good at holding back from giving too much-unsolicited advice.

It turned out that spending a week with my sister, Natalie, was the most effective lesson. With a nonverbal learning disability, she chooses her words carefully. She taught me that we can enjoy a puzzle or reading on the beach without chatting. She taught me the power of the thoughtful stare, and I am using it often these days. I could have saved a lot of time and energy this year by recognizing the teacher who was right before me.

So many of my friends are sending their kids off to college. I've become anxious over the limited time I have to force-feed my words of wisdom to these young men I have raised. I'm never quite sure if my sons heed my advice, but I try to have faith that some things will sink in if I keep sharing. I imagine I will blink and my time to impart my knowledge will have passed, so I jotted down a few notes.

Dear Sons,

There is so much I want to remind you of, but for now, I offer eight simple words of wisdom and pray that eight is enough.

1. Find the people who make you laugh and share your time with them.

2. Share your thoughts—both the light and dark ones. Often it can help your mindset if you get out of your own head and talk to people.

3. Share your joy. If you love a song, a movie, a place, or a book, tell others about it. They might also find enjoyment in the items you share.

4. Share your struggles. If you screw something up, do not hide from it, talk about it. The reality of the situation might not be as bad as you think. And if it truly is a horrible mistake, you can get help with your next steps.

5. Share your wallet—friends will never forget your generosity. Give back to the community around you as well. Little gift gestures can add up to make a big impact.

6. Share your dreams—you never know who you might inspire. You might also touch someone who can help you reach your dreams.

7. Spend your day on multiple interests—do not play one sport, read one book or listen to one song and make a judgment. Try many activities and hobbies because even the crummy ones might teach you something.

8. Share your heart—when you feel love for someone, tell them and show them often. Your heart might get hurt, but when it heals, it will beat with more strength.

And lastly, remember that we tell you we love you and care about you all the time, but we also tell you to change the toilet paper roll and put the dirty dishes directly into the dishwasher. I have practiced holding back so much unsolicited advice, but I want to share these words now, hoping the good stuff rises to the top.

Peace Train

"Do you hear them?" I ask Dale as he and Todd stand in our yard under the night stars.

"I can't hear anything, little lady," he replies as we hear hoots coming from the trees.

A little boy in our neighborhood picked up a feather on his walk with his mama.

"This means so much to me, I have so much hope now. I feel like it's a message from Owlivia's parents to say I love you."

I now look up at the sky on walks and search the treetops for nests. I listen intently for hoots, hoping the owls are creating new life.

When I was negotiating to leave my job I would rehearse what I was going to say in my car. It eased my nerves and increased my confidence as I drove. In one moment of self-doubt, I asked my Dad to show me a sign that I was making a smart decision. Madonna's "Like a Prayer," played on the radio. Summer of college when I would sleep in, my Dad would yell that I was "wasting the day away." He would drag a speaker to my bedroom door and blare the Madonna song. I accepted the job offer and thought it must have been a wonderful random coincidence that happened.

The day after my fifty-first birthday, I ran my first half-marathon through the streets of Boston. I passed Joy Street, then the spot where Todd proposed, where he asked my Dad if he could marry me, my first job, and the lunch spot I would meet my sister at when we were both starting out. It was nostalgic. At mile eleven I started to lose steam and as I passed my Dad's office building, I got emotional over how much I was missing him. I pulled out my phone and played music into my jog bra. Ally McBeal's soundtrack played, bringing me back to the '90s and the above memories. I would run these same streets with my sister and Dad. "I miss you so much, please send me a sign that you are with me," I said out loud (I was at a place where there weren't any runners around me). "I Will Find You," the Clannad song from his favorite *Last of the Mohicans* movie soundtrack played on my phone.

I ran the last mile with new power. I felt an incredible surge of joy and finished the last mile with my Dad by my side.

If you have recently joined me as a Grief Sister, know this: grieving is a trip without a roadmap, but you will eventually arrive at a good place. Just follow your own peace train.

Pour yourself a cup of coffee, and let's recap together:

1. If you don't stop to notice your surroundings, you might miss the magic.
2. Never lose your sense of wonder.
3. Celebrate those we have lost by enjoying the activities they did, recreating their recipes, and telling their stories to anyone who will listen.
4. Love a pet. A hamster, a dog, a pet rock, or an owl.
5. Find one burst of joy each day.
6. Send a text, make that call, write a letter, send a pigeon.
7. Find the humor. Do more of what or spend time with who makes you laugh.
8. Fill the gap.
9. When in doubt, use the cancer.
10. Joy is meant to be shared.

Gramma Phyllis's Rhubarb Pie

INGREDIENTS:

1 9-in pie crust

3 C rhubarb*

1 C sugar

1/8 tsp salt

3 tsp flour

2 eggs (beaten)

½ C raisins (cover with water and simmer until plump)

METHOD:

Preheat the oven to 425. Wash and cut rhubarb into ½-inch pieces before measuring. Mix sugar, flour, salt, and eggs. Add to the rhubarb and pour into the cooked pie crust. Sprinkle it with sugar and milk. Bake at 425 for 10 minutes. Reduce heat to 325 and continue baking for 10-15 min or until brown.

*When I make this pie, I save a small dish of the rhubarb mixture and freeze it into an ice cube tray. With a few sprigs of basil and soda water, it makes a refreshing vodka cocktail.

CHEERS!

Author's Journey

At thirteen, I wrote "The Story of My Life" and shared my dream to be a best-selling author and have a yacht (spelled "yot" so that intention was not set correctly). I wrote that the most important things in life were having a lot of friends, a loving family, and the ability to help people "share their money like Sally Struthers." Any meditation expert would say that I manifested my current life, minus the boat.

When I was a tween, I kept a diary with a small golden key to keep my stories safe. If I were angry at my Mom, upset with my sister, or had a crush on a boy, I would run to my bedroom to write it out. I wish I could see those entries today.

The year I was asked to quit ballet because I "lacked grace, balance and did not have the strength to advance," I wrote my debut storybook; *Susie and the Ballet Teacher*. What happened to the lesson of giving it your all? Practice makes perfect? Instead, I was taught "quit before you fall on your face." I don't remember talking to anyone about this devastating experience, but I did write a story about a mean ballet teacher. It was the '70s; children's psychology was not where it is today and no one analyzed my creative work. But at the tender age of eleven, I was given a gift that would stay with me my whole life in the form of a school project.

Butterflies danced in my stomach as I stood with my class-mates inside the Belmont Public Library, my Dorothy Hamil haircut pulled back in the ribbon barrettes I'd made in Girl Scouts. The librarian escorted us through the stacks, and there it was – *Susie and the Ballet Teacher*. I can still recall how I lit up seeing my book on the shelf and knew it was then I became inspired to use writing as a way of self-expression. I drew, I wrote diaries, I painted murals and I learned to share my stories.

As I got older, I worried my true feelings would be judged. I stopped writing in my diary, keeping my secrets safe inside. But when my Dad died, when my mom had cancer twice, when I struggled with infertility, and when I was a time-starved new mom, I turned to my journals. When I struggled with what to write, my therapist suggested I share my daily highs and lows and it helped me reframe many moments into positive reflections. Anytime things fell apart around me, I found handwriting my feeling to be therapeutic. I wrote two children's books when I wanted to explain those feelings to my sons. By sharing my creations, I was helping others who were struggling and that felt good.

For my forty-eighth birthday, which fell at the beginning of the pandemic, I bought myself *The Artist's Way*. The book's purpose is to open your blocked creativity by sticking to a daily writing practice. I started getting up five minutes earlier with a composition notebook. Months later, I became addicted to a daily writing practice. These were grave times for the world, and I wanted to help myself and my friends shift to a more positive mindset. Each day, I would write down a moment of joy that I felt. By sharing it, I would inspire others to go find their own joy. At a time when our energy was focused on viruses, I felt good making joy contagious.

Today, coffee and twenty minutes of writing each morning start my day with this meaningful meditation. It also gives me some me-time before the day takes over. Then again in the evening, I tuck myself into bed and write three things that I appreciate about the day. A laugh after a friend's message, a good dinner I cooked, or simply the fact that I am getting into bed early sends me to sleep in a positive mindset.

When we return from a vacation, I jot down the places we ate, stayed, and played. Recapping our adventures in my travel journal organizes the trip and I am able to give recommendations to friends, another joy burst in itself. I keep a small journal in my bag to capture ideas as they pop into my head. I use the notes feature on my phone since often the ideas come while out on a run, or in the shower and I don't have a pen nearby. I don't keep my diaries under lock and key anymore. Writing improves my mental health, one page at a time.

I have a deep love affair with books and have been a huge reader since I was an awkward tween. The characters in *Little House on the Prairie* were my friends when I didn't have many. Books were my escape and reading enabled me to travel to exotic places while my family never left the state of Massachusetts. I'd become so engrossed in the faraway location that I would forget that I had never flown on an airplane.

Sharing titles of books continues to be the way I connect with people from a wide range of ages and demographics. My go-to greeting is always "what are you currently reading?" I curate book lists and share them each season and it becomes the easiest way for me to connect with friends. Authors are the real heroes and yet they never know how many people they touch.

Thank you for reading this book and for passing it along to a friend when you are done. That is the best toast I can ask for.

XOXO,
Sami

Made in the USA
Middletown, DE
03 June 2023

31766382R00108